From
SCANDAL
to

From
SCANDAL
to

HOPE

Fr. Benedict J. Groeschel, C.F.R.

Our Sunday Visitor Publishing Division
Our Sunday Visitor, Inc.
Huntington, Indiana 46750

Our Sunday Visitor Publishing Division
Our Sunday Visitor, Inc.
200 Noll Plaza
Huntington, IN 46750

ISBN: 1-931709-69-6
LCCCN: 2002106849

Cover design by Eric Schoening
Cover image of Pope John Paul II is a
CNS photo from Reuters; used with permission
Interior design by Sherri L. Hoffman
Interior photos: Crucifix of San Damiano
by John Zierten; Shroud of Turin image from
Our Sunday Visitor photo files

PRINTED IN THE UNITED STATES OF AMERICA

This book attempts to make some sense of where we are to go now and is dedicated to:

The victims of sexual abuse and their families

The victims of misguided responses by Church authorities

The victims of false accusations

The victims of dissenting and inadequate religious teaching and relativism in moral theology

The victims of skeptical interpretations of Sacred Scripture

The great majority of the clergy, especially the Holy Father and the majority of bishops and superiors, whose loyalty and labor have been besmirched by the scandal

And finally to those who have the faith and courage to spend the rest of their lives in penance and reparation for what they did.

Carlo Carretto, an Italian spiritual writer in the latter part of the twentieth century, wrote these words in addressing his Church:

How much I must criticize you, my Church, and yet how much I love you. You have made me suffer more than anyone, and yet I owe more to you than anyone. I should like to see you destroyed, and yet I need your presence. You have given me much scandal, and yet you alone have made me understand holiness. Never in this world have I seen anything more compromised, more false, yet never have I touched anything more pure, more generous, and more beautiful.

Countless times I have felt like slamming the door of my soul in your face, and yet every night I have prayed that I might die in your sure arms. No, I cannot be free of you, for I am one with you, even if not completely you.

Then too . . . where would I go? To build another church? But I could not build one without the same defects, for they are my defects; and again, if I were to build another church, it would be my church, not Christ's Church. No, I am old enough. I know better.

— From *I Sought and I Found* (Maryknoll, N.Y.; Orbis Books, 1983)

CONTENTS

With Thanks   9

Preface: *By Most Reverend Timothy M. Dolan*   11

Chapter 1: *'You People Got a Lot of Trouble'*   15

Chapter 2: *Persecution*   41

Chapter 3: *An Urgent Appeal for Reform*   67

Chapter 4: *Reform Now!*   131

Epilogue   183

Prayers
   Prayer for the Church in Time of Scandal   187
   Prayer to Be Said by Victims and Their Families   189
   Prayer to Be Said by Priests Who Sinned
      Against the Young   191
   Prayer to Be Said by Those in Charge (Bishops,
      Superiors, and Their Assistants)   193
   Prayer to Be Said by Those Falsely Accused   195

Appendixes
   I. Pope John Paul II— *A Papal Address to the*
      Cardinals of the United States   199
   II. George Weigel — *Excerpts From the Series*
      'From Scandal to Reform'   204
   III. James O. Clifford, Sr. —*Double Standard in*
      Stories About Sexual Abuse   208
   IV. Johann Christoph Arnold — *Clergy*
      Sex Scandals Steal Headlines From
      Countless Faithful Who Defend Children
      and Uphold Chastity   213

WITH THANKS

This book obviously had to be written under great pressure of both time and responsibility. My motive for writing the book is to encourage Catholics toward the best use of the tremendous suffering we are all going through at this time. I am deeply grateful to Michael Dubruiel of Our Sunday Visitor and those who helped him. I'm especially indebted to that great optimist and my friend Bishop Timothy Dolan, who took the time out of his busy schedule to write a compelling Preface to this work.

I'm also deeply grateful to my friend Monsignor Peter Finn, rector of St. Joseph Seminary, Dunwoodie, Yonkers, New York, for reviewing the manuscript and making helpful suggestions.

As with so many of my books, this one could not have been written without the skilled and devoted editing of Charles Pendergast. He was assisted by my secretary June Pulitano, and by a most dedicated priest-volunteer who does much typing and wishes to remain unknown. I'm also deeply grateful to the priests, religious sisters and friars, and to the devout lay people who pray for our work.

FATHER BENEDICT J. GROESCHEL, C.F.R.
CORPUS CHRISTI, JUNE 2, 2002

PREFACE

Father Benedict Groeschel describes himself as "a New York moderate pessimist." Knowing Father Benedict as I do, I would submit that his self-description is overly pessimistic.

The Father Groeschel I know and admire is a man of profound faith. He is a man with a keen spiritual and pastoral sense. Over these many years, his books have called all of us to explore with greater depth and clarity our role as believers. Time and again, his writings call the Church to a critical reform and renewal, always consistent with the teachings of the Magisterium. His message, broadly interpreted, is one of great hope — hope in Christ's promise to be with us always. He may be a realist, but he's a priest of contagious hope.

We all are called to be people of hope. As an auxiliary bishop in the Archdiocese of St. Louis, I have been charged with overseeing the issue of those who allege sexual abuse by priests in our archdiocese. Over the past several months, I have met with victims and their families, who each display for me the pain and anger of terrible violation. I offer what support and assistance I can, and assure all to the best of my ability that no child will be at risk in our archdiocese. It is my prayerful hope that the Church will continue to progress in the way in which it addresses the needs of victims, charitably and pastorally.

I likewise have met with priests facing abuse allegations. While some of the allegations regrettably have proven true, others have not. Good priests in St. Louis and elsewhere have had their reputations sullied by false allegations. All priests, in fact, must deal on a daily basis with the societal perception — false though it may be — that "Catholic priest" equals "child abuser." The pain we all have faced during this difficult moment in the Church's history is enough to turn all of us into negative-minded pessimists! That's why this book is so welcome.

What is needed is context, and Father Groeschel provides it in this book. In his own unique and attractive style, Father Groeschel offers a kind of point-by-point lesson plan for renewal and purification in the Church. The renewal, he rightly notes, starts with individuals, who must recognize their important role as disciples. Through our own reading of Scripture, our prayer, our practice of virtue, and our reception of the sacraments, we more effectively can ascertain what role the Lord is asking us to play in shaping our society and our Church. As my ordinary here in St. Louis, Archbishop Justin Rigali, observes about the present crisis, "We can't get away with anything less than holiness, which shows itself in fidelity and integrity."

Prior to beginning my service as an auxiliary bishop, I served for seven years as rector of the Pontifical North American College in Rome. During my tenure in Rome, I came to know hundreds of happy, healthy, holy men who have become faithful priests. So much about these men gives cause for optimism: their willingness to say "yes" to God's call; the zeal with which they undertook their studies; and the profound joy one could see in their faces as they were ordained to the holy priesthood. Even a New York pessimist would have cause to smile!

As you read Father Groeschel's book, remember to smile! Remember that the victory has been won! Remember that the gates of hell shall not prevail against Christ's Church! Remember that

all things are possible with God! But solemnly remember, too, the important and continuing role
we all must play to make His light of truth visible
to all. It is a task we must take on with the utmost
seriousness.

MOST REVEREND TIMOTHY M. DOLAN
AUXILIARY BISHOP OF ST. LOUIS

One

'YOU PEOPLE GOT A LOT OF TROUBLE'

Unexpectedly, out of the blue, the Catholic Church in the United States and in the other English-speaking countries is facing its greatest challenge in at least two hundred years. Here in the United States, the Church is humiliated and demoralized. The bishops are shaken. Priests are discouraged. Many of the most loyal Catholics are angry at Church authorities, and everyone wonders what will happen. This is a time, then, to turn to God. This should not be seen merely as a pious thought, but as a very real demand of the times.

In this book, we want to look at the problem that has been in the media day after day. And at the same time, we want to look at the media's attack on the Church, which this problem has occasioned. There's a feeding frenzy by media sharks against the Catholic Church, and they have their reasons. Finally, we want to look for solutions that may be found in this suffering, to see what can be done to bring good out of this situation.

Terence Cardinal Cooke, the late Archbishop of New York, who is now proposed for beatification, used to say, "There are no problems; there are just challenges." He was a great optimist. I am not. I'm a New York moderate pessimist, but somehow or other the Cardinal and I got along. Even a pessimist like myself, however, can see in the present crisis many opportunities for evangelization and, in fact, for the purification of the Church.

One of the bishops who is being ripped to pieces in the media, a good and devout man who made some big mistakes (or at least his associates did), wrote to me recently, "I know that Our Lord is with us in these dark times, and that at the end of the day this will lead to a purification of the Church."

Let's look at the present scandal. I have looked for someone we can depend on for the facts, without the smoke and hysteria of the media. I have found someone who is not a member of the Catholic Church — Professor Philip Jenkins, a very respected scholar and professor of history and religious studies at Pennsylvania State University. He is the author of *Pedophiles and Priests: Anatomy of a Contemporary Crisis* (Oxford University Press, 1996). I'll quote from his book and also from a recent interview he had with my friends John Burger and Kathryn Jean Lopez in the *National Catholic Register*.

The Victims and the Penitent

Let me say at the very beginning that none of my remarks fails to take into account the anguish, anger, and hurt of victims, their parents, families, and friends. I am very sensitive to the victims. For almost thirty years, my full-time job has been working with priests as a spiritual director, counselor, and, at times, psychotherapist. I am working with some volunteers, a few of whom are relatives of victims, to see if we can begin a prayer movement to bring some spiritual healing to these people, who have a right to expect help from the Church.

As a psychologist for priests, I have occasionally spoken to the victims of priests and to their families. I can only say that I am deeply, deeply grieved. I often had to accept their anger, not directed personally at me, but at Church authorities. I did not like this experience, but I accepted it because of my firm belief that Christ founded the Catholic Church. With Him and in Him, I am willing to suffer with the victims.

One bishop described himself as "anguished" by what the victims said. I think that the vast majority of priests, including some of those who are accused and some who are guilty, are filled with disappointment and anguish. I also know those who have done these things, and some of them are among the most penitent people I've ever met in my whole life.

When you pick up a newspaper, listen to the radio, or watch television news, the media don't tell you about the penitent priests. I can mention the case of Archbishop Eugene Marino, who about fourteen years ago had to resign as Archbishop of Atlanta in a scandal. At that time, I realized that when a scandal occurs, about two percent of what is said in the media is true.

For those who are unfamiliar with this case, Archbishop Marino, America's first black archbishop, was reported to have had an affair with a woman. While I do not wish to go into the case, the media cast the situation in an entirely false light.

I saw Archbishop Marino a week or so before his death, because he was required to check with me once a month. He lived a life of extreme humiliation, humility, and penitence. He was a most humble man. Shortly before his death, some bishop-friends took him to see the Pope. The Archbishop never ran away from who he really was. For those who remember, his name was synonymous with scandal. He once said to me, "I've scandalized half a billion people."

During the official visit with the Holy Father, Archbishop Marino came up with some other bishops, introduced himself directly, and said, "Your Holiness, I am Archbishop Marino."

The Pope looked at him and said, "Your Excellency, I know who you are. I have a question. Are you at peace?"

Archbishop Marino replied, "Yes, Holy Father. I am at peace."

The Pope embraced him and said, "Thanks be to God."

While one deeply, deeply sympathizes with the victims, one must never refuse someone the opportunity for repentance. This is especially true if that person has failed in the pursuit of a challenging and difficult vocation like celibacy. I don't think anyone was ever ordained with the idea of causing sexual scandal or of betraying the promise of chastity, but in the difficult and confusing years of the last three decades (which I will attempt to trace), these things have happened. It should be no surprise that we priests are affected by the world we live in. In America, we live in a corrupt culture that is slipping rapidly into paganism.

The Council and the Cultural Revolution

The good news of the Second Vatican Council (1962–1965) broke on the world at a time of cultural upheaval and revolution.[1] Most of us are not as aware of that revolution as we might be. A fair amount of this revolution was caused by an ill-advised application of psychology. In his 1975 presidential address, Professor Donald Campbell, president of the American Psychological Association, denounced the profession of psychology for undermining the moral values of eighty to ninety percent of college undergraduates by teaching the erroneous idea that pleasure was the best guide to development and happiness.[2]

I spoke to Campbell not long before his death a few years ago, and I asked him if he still had the same convictions.

He answered, "No, I think it's worse than I said at that time."

Psychology and psychiatry are big words. They include many things. Among the great psychologists of history are Sts. Augustine, Bonaventure, Teresa of Ávila, John of the Cross, and Ven. John Henry Cardinal Newman. Psychology simply means the study of the functioning of the human mind. Some of the great psychologists of modern times made some big mistakes, especially Sigmund Freud. Along with many others, Freud was a materialist. He denied that human beings have any spiritual component at all, and he seriously thought of us as well-developed and complex apes. Personally, he was a better man than his philosophy might suggest. He was not a badly behaved man; however, he was rather depressed, and considering his views, I don't blame him.

Despite his blind materialism, Freud and those who followed him had an incredible effect on society. The theories of Freud and others reached most people in a kind of watered-down way. It was believed that the only way an individual could be mature in general, or sexually mature in particular, was to be sexually unrepressed. If you push the theory a step further, people were immature unless they were sexually experienced and involved. Without this sexual involvement, there was no hope for maturity.

In Freud's defense, it must be said that he was not thinking of celibate clergy when he proposed his theory. Later, Erik Erikson, one of the eminent psychological writers who attempted to "baptize" Freud, actually made explicit allowance for a person to be chaste and celibate and yet mature. But this was not particularly noticed in the field.[3]

Some of the very people who uncritically accepted these ideas are on television right now. They are usually ex-priests telling the Church what to do and denouncing its traditions. Considering that some of them are themselves responsible for the thinking that led to this catastrophe, a touch of class might have suggested that they keep quiet. I refer here particularly to Richard Sipe and Eugene Kennedy.

The Third Way

Kennedy was responsible for a theory called the "third way," which meant that those vowed to chastity could have warm, close, emotionally expressive relationships with members of the opposite sex and nothing would happen. As someone from Jersey City, I thought the whole idea very funny and very tragic at the same time. Kennedy and Paul F. D'Arcy wrote a book called *The Genius of the Apostolate: Personal Growth in the Candidate, the Seminarian and the Priest* (Sheed and Ward, 1965). They proposed the third way as an answer to many problems confronted by priests, ignoring the fact that the same problems were often encountered with people from all walks of life and other religious traditions.

In 1970, I was working as an intern in Psychiatric Institute, where one of my colleagues was a tough Jewish guy from Brooklyn who was a psychiatrist in training. He came up to me one day and said to me, "Hey, Benedict, did you ever hear of this book?" And he waved a copy of *The Genius of the Apostolate* in front of me.

I replied, "Not only did I hear of it; I know the people who wrote it."

My friend said, "Is this a satire? Is it a joke?"

I said, "No, they're very serious," and I remember what he said to me: "You people got a lot of trouble."

Those words are echoing in my ears, even now, thirty years later.

As a result of the tidal wave of influences similar to the ideas of Kennedy and D'Arcy, many priests left the priesthood. In those days, I interviewed 400 priests who left the ministry, as Kennedy and D'Arcy themselves did. I've written the psychological part of the petition for dispensation for 184 priests; happily, 85 priests have returned to the active ministry through our Trinity Retreat House of the New York Archdiocese.

While the third way was going on and priests were leaving to get married, something even more damaging was going on in the Church. That was the emergence of a gay subculture in American society. There have always been people with homosexual tendencies, which simply means an attraction for a person of the same sex. Some homosexual people have never once misbehaved in their lives. I suspect that some of them may be among the canonized saints. Homosexual tendencies in themselves never hurt anybody.

Sexual dysfunctions, like all other human problems, can be a cross, a painful opportunity for virtue and growth in the spiritual life. As children of a fallen race, human beings have always endured sexual problems or dysfunctions. Many of these — like sadism, masochism, and compulsive promiscuity — are common in heterosexual people as well. Sexual conflicts do not hurt people; what hurts people is sin. So while some people were misbehaving heterosexually, Americans were accepting premarital intercourse, fornication, and adultery — all of which have been encouraged in the media, especially in films and television, for many years. The fact is that movies up to the late 1950s celebrated virtue, including chastity, and now they celebrate vice. While all this was taking place, people with homosexual tendencies who were involved in that behavior "came out of the closet," so to speak, and the Western world developed the "gay scene."

The Gay Scene

The word "gay" in this context means a lifestyle that is contrary to the Bible (see the Letter to the Romans, chapter 1), to the traditional teachings of the Catholic Church and of many other Christian churches, as well as to many other religious faiths up until the mid-twentieth century. Christianity has nothing directly to say about homosexual tendencies, which are a misfortune, and, if possible, may be dealt with as a cross. Christianity, when it is properly taught, condemns all sinful behavior, but not the sinner. Its founder, Jesus Christ, said, "I did not come to judge the world but to save the world" (John 12:47).

There are many forms of sexual activity that are forbidden by Christian tradition as well as by Judaism, from which our faith comes. This particular problem has become a scene, a lifestyle, and a subculture. As Professor Jenkins — who is not a Catholic — and any number of others have pointed out, the present scandal involving clergy is not about pedophilia. It is about active homosexuality with minors.

In his book, Jenkins reviews a study of more than twenty-two hundred priests of the Archdiocese of Chicago during a forty-year period. Of those twenty-two hundred priests, only one had been convicted of pedophilia.[4] Pedophilia is sexual activity with a prepubescent youngster, a child. After puberty, sexual activity with a young person is just as illegal and immoral, but it's either homosexual or heterosexual fornication. It is especially wrong because it violates both the rights of a youngster to protection from such things and the rights of the young person's parents. This type of fornication is also a grave sin against charity because it induces the young person into sin. The media are calling it "pedophilia," but that's a phony name. In all my years working as a psychologist, I have talked to two people with pedophile tendencies, and they had never acted out these impulses, which they recognized with horror. They stayed far away from every occasion of sin.

This scandal is about a form of homosexuality. I'm sorry to say that in the confusion that resulted after the Second Vatican Council (but not because of the Council), gay behavior and the acting out of homosexual tendencies gradually and subtly became accepted in various sectors of different churches, including my own. I stress this fact because a person may be homosexually oriented and at the same time perfectly chaste and perfectly well-behaved. These devout people are not gay or lesbians, since these two terms refer to people who embrace a lifestyle that is at odds with Christian belief and morality.

Many heterosexual people have masochistic tendencies, sadistic tendencies, or both. Others may be voyeurs — people who look at others lustfully and compulsively. They may have other problems as well. In 1985, I wrote a book called *The Courage to Be Chaste* (Paulist Press). My initial intention was to write for people who belong to a Catholic organization called Courage, which encourages homosexually oriented people to lead a chaste life. And they do. Courage has spread throughout the English-speaking world.

Later I decided to broaden the scope of my book to include all those who thought of themselves as permanently unmarried, including the widowed and divorced. I discussed various sexual pathologies in the book, but I never discussed pedophilia, because it didn't appear to be a problem. I did discuss homosexuality, but members of the gay scene were only beginning to become a vocal minority. Even today, validly conducted polls among adult males report that less than three percent of respondents identify themselves as active homosexuals. Only gradually in the 1980s were Americans becoming aware that there was a spreading involvement of teenagers in the homosexual behavior of adults.

Some of the confusion here comes from the legal definition of pedophilia, which includes sexual activity with any person below the legal age of maturity, which varies from state to state, from sixteen to eighteen years of age. It is interesting that right now, while all this havoc is going on, some self-styled liberal organizations in the United States are trying to lower or abolish the minimum age for legal sexual behavior. Some important people in the previous presidential administration are countenancing this movement, which would legalize sexual behavior for any child, as they have legalized abortion for minors without parental consent.

The Media Blitz

Now I come to the big question about the media: Does anyone think that Catholic clergy are the only people who have this problem? People in the media apparently believe that they are. I've been around a long time. Various religious denominations, schools, youth services, social services, family services, military services, organizations for youth — they all encounter the same problem, as does the Catholic Church, and they all have generally handled it in the same way. They have very rarely brought cases of sexual misconduct with minors into criminal court for the simple reason that their families did not want to do so. They did not want to put the youngster before a court, and so these things were settled most often with the knowledge of district attorneys, and with the involvement of lawyers, along with the payment of considerable sums in damages. In other words, they acted exactly the same as the Catholic bishops are accused of doing things right now.[5]

The religious denominations and youth service organizations involved in these cases were almost always represented by the attorneys in the employ of the insurance companies that paid all or part of the damages. I think that many bishops and religious superiors realize in retrospect that they made a bad mistake by not meeting with the victims and their families. There may have been a pastoral obligation to do so. Because these cases were seen as adversarial proceedings, lawyers followed the rule of strongly discouraging or even forbidding the Church authorities from meeting with the victims and their families.

The Role of Psychology

Another big mistake was made in dealing with the offending clergy. The religious authorities regret now that they listened so easily to the advice of psychiatrists and psychologists, who actually had little experience in dealing with adults who were sexually involved with minors. Psychiatrists and psychologists thought they knew more than they did. I've been involved in psychology for four decades, and we in the profession were naïve enough to think that these offenders could almost always be cured. Often the families were satisfied with treatment of the offender, because it is generally known that the most common forum in which pedophilia occurs is the family itself. Families of victims also thought that offenders within the family could be cured. Frequently, the families wisely insisted that offenders who had been treated would not work with minors in the future. As a matter of fact, a great many offenders did profit very well from successful treatment, although I'm not sure that you can say offenders are cured. It would be more accurate to say that a sexual attraction to children or teenagers can be arrested and controlled. In many cases, some of the people who are named in the newspapers right now were successfully treated long ago and have been out of treatment for twenty or twenty-five years. They have done very good work. Others who were not Catholic clergy function in different denominations, organizations, or groups, and for the most part they still function in their own families. Sexual problems of any kind have not reoccurred in many cases, especially when treatment was joined by a powerful sense of conversion and contrition. This kind of treatment is very similar to that of twelve-step groups, which include a real experience of moral conversion and repentance.

It is interesting to ask why Catholics are being singled out by the media. I know a number of very serious cases involving non-Catholic clergy that were handled out of court. No one seems to call that a cover-up.

Jenkins made the point very well when he was asked, "Is the Catholic Church getting an unfair rap in the media?" Jenkins said, "I think so, both in the exclusive focus on the Catholic side of things, and the exaggeration of what they are supposed to have done [by using the word "pedophiles"]. I am also shocked by the disingenuous neglect of the legal factors involved in all these cases, and the suggestion that the lawyers representing the victims are always crusaders for truth and justice. A lot are sharks, pure and simple, who shamelessly exploit the media to promote anticlerical stereotypes."[6] I want to repeat that Jenkins is not a Catholic.

Wasted Suffering?

Bishop Fulton Sheen used to say, "There's nothing worse than wasted suffering." The Church is suffering — clergy, laity, religious, the whole Church together, especially parents and children and, most of all, victims and their families. Everyone is suffering. Let's not waste suffering, because scandal can be a wake-up call for the reform of the Church in the United States. The Franciscan Friars and Sisters of the Renewal have thought for fifteen years that the Catholic Church needs reform. This means that we all need personal reform from within. But this particular scandal gives us an excellent opportunity to examine the collective conscience of the Church and face its severe critics, many of whom are motivated by a hatred of religion and a hatred of the Catholic Church because it is the loudest voice of religion and morality in our country.

Holy Church/Worldly Church

Active American Catholics and most of the publications they produce and read would give the impression that Catholicism is thriving in the United States of America. The fact is that attendance at Mass has dramatically fallen off in the last generation. Some take consolation in the fact that this is true in other denominations as well; however, it is not true of Evangelical Protestants and Orthodox Jews.

Membership in religious communities has declined catastrophically, and enrollment in Catholic seminaries is alarmingly small in relation to the perceived needs of the future. Despite all this, you could read various Catholic publications and never know that we were having a problem. Even the annual meetings of the bishops or of other national Catholic organizations reflect an attitude that suggests fiddling while Rome burns. I must confess to being part of that attitude myself at times. I'm not pointing fingers at anyone in particular, but at all of us in general.

Those who feel that they have the responsibility of identifying the problems often do so in such caustic terms that those they want to reach will not listen to them. As a rule, those who are very critical of the present situation in the Church have their own particular panacea, which may range from Latin liturgy to the ordination of women. None of these issues really touches the heart of the problem.

The heart of the problem is that we have become a worldly Church. We are filled with many worldly ideas that we have absorbed from the general culture. This is much more true now that we are no longer a minority group. Catholic colleges, universities, and other institutions, as well as the Catholic clergy themselves, remained rather separated from the declining culture by our own well-expressed values up to the time of the Second Vatican Council, which came soon after the election of the first and only Catholic president of the United States.

Theoretically, we moved out of the Catholic ghetto, which was hampering us. Many thought, rather unrealistically, that the world around us was just waiting with open arms to receive the newly upholstered Catholic identity of the Second Vatican Council. Although everyone seemed to join in the chorus of jubilation, it cannot be said that the Catholic Church has affected society positively or outstandingly in the past thirty or forty years. Our imports from the secular culture vastly outnumber our exports to it, indicating, in a kind of financial symbolism, that our balance of trade is way off.

Despite a great deal of talk about spirituality, anyone really familiar with the spiritual literature of the Catholic Church can see that in recent decades we have not been living up to that literary tradition; rather, an alarming decline in spirituality has been evident in American Catholicism. Christian spirituality calls for the cultivation of virtue and the avoidance of sin in the spiritual journey to God. It calls for a complete reliance on the grace of Christ for salvation and sanctification. An incredible array of psychological and cultural gimmicks has come to replace serious spirituality. Psychological techniques, many of them lacking any scientific verification, have replaced the examination of conscience. All kinds of little enterprises borrowed from New Age spirituality, ranging from labyrinths to massage retreats, have taken the place of solid spiritual exercises. Sometimes you wonder: Are we running a Church or a circus?

A review of Catholic religious education books over the years shows an unbelievable superficiality, although all involved were trying hard to match the techniques of secular education. Religious educators may get a high grade for effort, but they certainly will not get a high grade for results.

Catholic higher education is in an appalling state. An honest list of those institutions of higher education that are both dynamic and orthodox would be very short. A slightly longer list of Catholic colleges really trying to hang on to their Catholic identity could also be drawn up. However, as we shall see later in this book, the picture of Catholic religious education in particular, and of Catholic education in general, is disgraceful.

Shall we speak of the decline of the priesthood and religious life? There are many good and excellent priests and many devout religious. There are also any number of them who take their responsibilities in a lackadaisical way and seem to be proud of it. They expect people to applaud them because they think they are "with it," as part of the overall American culture. Then there are those whose real affiliation with the Catholic

Church and its clerical or religious life is simply an act of hypocrisy. They don't mean to be hypocrites, because that would take just a bit more religious conviction than they actually have. They sail along under the banner of the Church but have absolutely no intention of listening to it, following its prescriptions, living up to the expectations of its members, or fulfilling its obligations. For some religious, the only visible evidence that they belong to consecrated life is that they are tax-exempt once a year.

The present disaster and scandal reveal that there has been much relativistic moral theology and practice. A great many priests and religious have held out against moral relativism, with varying degrees of certitude; but it has crept in nonetheless. This relativism has been most influential perhaps because most people are unaware of it and think that it simply comes through the media and television itself. A priest living alone in a one-man parish — or a religious returning to his or her apartment or to a small religious community where everyone lives a very independent life — will find some relaxation in the evening watching television. However, the values pouring out of the media are worldly, materialistic, antihuman, and anti-Christian.

The whole idea that a Christian is called on to reject the spirit of the world is lost. Such biblical texts as "The ruler of this world is coming [but he] has no power over me" (John 14:30) and "For all that is in the world, the lust of the flesh and the lust of the eyes and the pride of life, is not of the Father but is of the world" (1 John 2:16) are no longer part of the spiritual consciousness of Catholics. The many definitive and caustic sermons of Jesus Christ against worldliness and the spirit of the world are completely abandoned in favor a mindless embrace of secular humanism. And secular humanism itself has reached a level of degradation that would embarrass even the early-twentieth-century secular humanist, who had at least a modicum of dignity, unlike his counterpart of today.

Now is a time for reform. It must begin on all sides, and people have to clamor for it. Bishops will have to clamor among bishops, priests among priests, religious brothers and sisters among the members of their communities, and devout Catholic laity in their own parishes. In fact, every person who wishes to see the United States return to being a moral nation should join in this clamor. Otherwise, we are in irreversible decline.

This is the question before every member of the clergy, every religious, and every layperson interested in being a real Christian: Are we going to follow Jesus Christ and the Gospel, or are we going to follow the spirit of the world and continue to decline into moral, religious, and cultural chaos?

When I look at this dismal scene and survey the confusion and betrayal of our contemporary Church, I can only say that now is a time when we must turn to God. But each one of us must turn to Him with all our heart and follow His commandments and the teachings of our Lord Jesus Christ wholeheartedly and without compromise.

Endnotes

1. See Gerald Arbuckle, *Strategies for Growth in Religious Life* (New York: Alba House, 1986), for a comprehensive review of this cultural revolution; see also Benedict J. Groeschel, C.F.R., *The Reform of Renewal* (San Francisco: Ignatius Press, 1990), p. 143.

2. See Paul Vitz, *Psychology as Religion: The Cult of Self-Worship* (Grand Rapids, Mich.: Eerdmans, 1975), p. 49; see also Groeschel, *The Reform of Renewal*, p. 96.

3. See Erik Erikson, *Childhood and Society* (New York: W.W. Norton, 1963), p. 267.

4. Philip Jenkins, *Pedophiles and Priests: Anatomy of a Contemporary Crisis* (New York: Oxford University Press, 1996), p. 82.

5. See Appendix III.

6. John Burger and Kathryn Jean Lopez, "Media Myths Fuel the Clergy Abuse Scandal," *National Catholic Register*, April 7-13, 2002.

Two

PERSECUTION

It is quite amazing that even when persecutions are taking place, many are unaware of them. We are probably only slightly aware of the persecution of Christians in Sudan going on at present. If you don't read Catholic publications, you may not even know about it. Thousands and thousands of people have been killed in the past two decades because they were Christians. Most people are vaguely aware of the persecution of many forms of Christianity and religion in general in China, but they shrug their shoulders. Too bad, they say. Maybe trading with China will make it all go away. Maybe.

How many Catholics know that, with the support of the American government, the Mexican anticlerical Masonic government killed hundreds of priests in Mexico in 1928? Some of these murdered priests were recently beatified, joining the Jesuit martyr Blessed Miguel Pro. Most people are aware of the Communist persecution of the Church but know very little about Hitler's persecution and its gigantic scope. Only a few weeks before this writing, I knelt at the door of the cell where Maximilian Kolbe was starved to death. On that holy spot, I prayed to him, thinking of the media blitz against the Catholic Church right now, which has gotten worse even in those few weeks.

We gain some insight into the media blitz and its purposes from the following quotation of Adolf Hitler in 1937, someone whom I've never quoted before: "The Third Reich does not desire a *modus vivendi* [a way of getting along] with the Catholic Church, but rather its destruction with lies and dishonor."[1]

The Nazis prosecuted one hundred seventy Franciscans in 1937 on the trumped-up charge of running a male brothel. All together, one thousand religious were put into jail in Germany just on those false charges.

Speaking about Catholics, Hitler also said:

> I shall make them appear ridiculous and contemptible. I shall order films to be made about them. . . . Let the whole mass of nonsense, selfishness, repression, and deceit be revealed: how they drained money out of the country . . . how they committed incest. We shall make it so thrilling that everyone will want to see it. There will be queues outside the cinemas.[2]

On Good Friday, I was getting ready to go to preach the three hours when the wife of a very dear friend of mine, Rabbi David Blumenthal, came to my office with her adult son. Ursula and Philip apologized that the rabbi couldn't come because it was Passover. They wanted to express the solidarity of their family with all the Catholic clergy and me. They thought what the media were doing was horrible. As she was leaving, Ursula said to me, "They're doing this to you now. What will they do when they turn on us?" This is a very real question. The media blitz against the Catholic Church may be the first of many.

The media have become a monster in the United States. I use the word "media" in a general way. Obviously, there are better and worse forms of the media. But as someone who has been around the media for twenty years, I can tell you that, as a rule, the last question that is asked is "What is truth?" There was a time when the ideal of journalism was to present the truth. Americans today hardly know what truth is.

We are saturated with advertising from the time we are little children. We receive messages all day long to buy things we don't need and can't use, and which will probably kill us if we use them long enough. "Welcome to Marlboro Country." How many times have we looked at those stupid pictures of the cowboy smoking a cigarette? By this time, the cowboy is probably dead. The horse, too. No doubt the horse developed cancer from the secondary smoke of the cowboy's cigarettes.

We are experiencing a media blitz right now against the Catholic Church. Why? They seemed to be our friends only a short while ago. Now they have very good reasons to attack us. In the early 1990s, an opinion poll was conducted among media personnel in California. Over ninety percent of those involved in the media establishment were in favor of equating homosexual relationships with traditional marriage. Considerably more than ninety percent were in favor of abortion-on-demand. That's why they consider us their enemies. Their goal is not to bother the people who say the Rosary or come to Benediction. Their goal is to destroy any public influence that the Catholic Church or its bishops might have. That's their goal, and they are succeeding very well in reaching it.

Professor Philip Jenkins, whom we referred to in the last chapter, writing recently in a newspaper article, exposed the lies and distortions of the media attack on the Church. Jenkins, who you will recall is not a Catholic, stated, "Every day the news media have a new horror story to report, under some sensational headline: *Newsweek*, typically, is devoting its current front cover to 'Sex, Shame and the Catholic Church: 80 Priests Accused of Child Abuse in Boston.' " It is important to remember that some of the accusations were made against priests who are no longer alive. Others are no longer priests, and many of the cases wouldn't stand up if they ever went to court. Jenkins went on to say that while the "Boston church authorities committed dreadful errors," the current scandal "should not be used to launch blanket accusations against the Catholic Church as a whole."[3]

Celibacy and Chastity

There are a number of Catholics who dumbly get on the bandwagon. There are two groups of Catholics that should be embarrassed. One is a group often referred to as liberal Catholics, who claim that the scandal proves that we should get rid of celibacy, that we should perhaps get rid of the priesthood itself. Jenkins has said, "My research of cases over the past 20 years indicates no evidence whatever that Catholic and other celibate clergy are any more likely to be involved in misconduct or abuse than clergy of any other denomination — or indeed, than non-clergy. However determined news media may be to see this affair as a crisis of celibacy, the charge is just unsupported."[4]

Members of the other group, who consider themselves traditional Catholics, have been scathing and disrespectful of the bishops and even of the Holy Father. In doing so, they actually contradict many of their own values, which include a respect for authority.

Even Treatment for All?

Literally every denomination and faith tradition has its share of abuse cases, and some of the worst have involved non-Catholics. There was a case in New York a few years ago of four clergymen of the same denomination charged with setting up a ring of boys brought up from the Caribbean for the purpose of sexual involvement. There was a small article in the back pages of the local newspaper. What would we have heard if these clergy had been Catholic priests?

A few years ago, I sadly read in a very responsible Evangelical Protestant publication, *Christianity Today*, that two ministers — one of a well-known church, the other of a smaller church — had been accused in the same month of murdering their wives. I won't mention the names of the churches because I am sure they don't approve of their ministers killing their wives. And I don't know whether they killed their wives or not, but they were indicted, according to this small notice. Suppose a Catholic priest killed someone. Would you hear about it? Did you ever hear about these ministers? If they had been priests, you would have heard about it on the front page, day after day. *The Boston Globe* published scores of articles on its front page on the subject of James Porter, who had been dismissed years earlier from the priesthood. The *Globe* insisted on continually calling him "Father." *The Boston Globe* has probably the longest history of anti-Catholicism of any newspaper in the United States. And it goes on.

Although it is difficult to get statistics, I understand that a survey was done in which it was stated that seventy-nine clergy in the United States are in prison at this writing for "legal" pedophilia — that is, sexual behavior with a person under legal age. Probably almost all of the cases were with teenagers. Forty of the seventy-nine are Protestant ministers. This is not surprising since a majority of the clergy in the United States are Protestant. The rest are divided between Catholics, Orthodox, Jews, and other clergy. I think it is rather clear to anybody who reads the papers that there is a media blitz against the Catholic Church, especially with some papers that claim respectability, like *The New York Times*.

Bill Keller, a writer for *The New York Times Magazine*, achieved new lows of anti-Catholicism on May 4, 2002. In an op-ed article, he accused the Pope of replicating "something very like the old Communist Party in his church." He went on to say that "Karol Wojtyla has shaped a hierarchy that is intolerant of dissent, unaccountable to its members, secretive in the extreme and willfully clueless about how people live." He said that the Vatican "exists first and foremost to preserve its own power." He accused the Pope of having "carefully constructed a Kremlin that will be inhospitable to a reformer." He repeatedly committed the outrage of comparing the Pope to Leonid Brezhnev, the late Communist dictator. He also accused the Pope of making seminaries "factories of conformity, begetting a generation of inflexible young priests who have no idea how to talk to real-life Catholics."[5]

Seldom in the history of journalism have I seen such virulent attacks on any institution that is supposed to receive fair treatment in the press. Although Keller confesses himself to be a "collapsed Catholic," he is a Catholic in no sense of the word at all, while pretending to have some interest in Catholicism. He misconstrues and misrepresents the Pope's teaching and positions in the most crude and vicious way. One could not care less about what Bill Keller thinks; but that a respectable newspaper would allow itself to be the purveyor of such vicious anti-Catholic propaganda is beginning to put that publication in the same category as a magazine favoring the Ku Klux Klan or the League of the Militant Godless.

Another article, titled "The Vatican Rag," by Maureen Dowd (who also claims to be a Catholic and is a regular editorial writer for the op-ed page of *The New York Times*), suggests some real personal problems centered around the Church and its teaching. She appears to have a deep emotional bias against the Pope.

> The pope cited "our brothers" who had succumbed to "mysterium iniquitatis (the mystery of evil)." Calling it the mystery of evil vaporizes the problem. There's nothing very mysterious about pedophilia. It's a crime. . . .
>
> The Vatican's reaction can be summed up this way: Priests don't abuse boys. Americans do. The Vatican has shrugged off the international spate of sex abuse cases and acted as if this is another overhyped American tabloid sex scandal. . . .
>
> The Vatican's cavalier attitude will only intensify the collision between the open, modernizing spirit of America and the deeply anti-democratic spirit of the church. . . .
>
> And American boomers, who see the Vatican's precepts on sex and virtue as frozen and antiquated, have become "cafeteria Catholics," selecting dishes from the Vatican *prix fixe* menu and circumnavigating bans on premarital sex, birth control, and divorce.[6]

Throughout the country, newspapers carry articles like these, which are a gross insult to hundreds of thousands of their readers. Many of the writers claim to be Catholic, but like Keller, Dowd, and Frances Kissling of Catholics for a Free Choice, they appear to be on their way out of the Church. They claim to represent a Catholic constituency that does not actually exist. I'm suggesting to my readers: cancel your subscriptions to anti-Catholic newspapers, magazines, and other publications, but do it with a letter. If you need to see the ads, borrow yesterday's paper from your neighbors who are nice agnostics, or access them on the Internet, where you really don't give them any support.

The striking paradox is that while the media are heaping insult on the Catholic Church and the Catholic clergy, the worst example of corrupting the morals of minors in the United States that everyone knows about is television aimed at teenagers. I received a report recently of the financial status of a television network that is aimed entirely at teenagers. I don't wish to give the name, but you probably know what I'm talking about. A friend of mine, a former minister, watched the network for one day at my request and found that the sponsors included a number of well-known corporations. These programs corrupt the morals of immense numbers of minors. Why are the networks able to do it? Because they have the protection of the Supreme Court. So do abortionists, who perform abortions on minors without the consent of parents. Is any voice raised in protest? Yet, we are overwhelmed by the media blitz aimed exclusively at the Catholic clergy.

A number of Catholics are annoyed at me for pointing out that the news media are dishonestly and unfairly singling out the Catholic clergy. I maintain that radio, press, and television give a disproportionate amount of coverage to scandals involving Catholic clergy and play down or completely ignore the problem of sexual abuse of minors in other areas of American life. This gives the widely held impression that only Catholics are experiencing this scandal. Fairness in reporting requires some sense of proportion. The media also concentrate on the message that Catholic authorities have done nothing, while at the same time they are trumpeting the fact that the Church (actually its insurance companies) has paid large settlements. Both of these cannot be true at the same time. James O. Clifford, Sr., a former reporter for United Press International and Associated Press, reveals this dishonesty of the media who are obsessed with the scandal in the Catholic Church while ignoring the same problems in public education. He sees the problem in terms of shoddy journalism in some cases, but the disparity in handling cases against the Catholic Church is so blatant that shoddy journalism can be only part of the story. The fact is that all organizations caring for youths have tended to deal with these cases involving minors in exactly the same way. I suggest you read Clifford's article in Appendix III.

Clerical Psychopaths

To be sure, Church authorities have made terrible mistakes. The media would like you to believe that the bishops were unconcerned about these issues. Some bishops were mistaken, and at times these terrible mistakes led to things that are terrifying and lamentable. Innocent youngsters were badly hurt and so were their families. I can tell you from personal experience that in the last thirty years no single problem has occupied the attention of bishops and religious administrators more than clerical misbehavior. This problem has taken up more attention than even the one of priests leaving the priesthood. The bishops listened to lawyers and to psychologists, psychiatrists, and others in the behavioral sciences, who often were correct in their assessments but who were sometimes tragically wrong about a particular case.

How did the serial pedophilia cases ever occur? I am convinced that the most egregious cases occurred in the lives of those who are psychopaths. Psychopaths are people who can lie time after time and not know they're doing it. Years ago there was a popular novel by Sinclair Lewis called *Elmer Gantry*. It was the story of a minister who was a psychopath. Talleyrand, the excommunicated Bishop of Autun, in France, was probably the world's most famous psychopath. He ended up being the most excommunicated person in history. He became a bishop purely for political reasons, through an appointment by the king. He never spent a day in a seminary and did untold damage to the Church. There's nobody more dangerous than a clerical psychopath. Certainly, the serial offenders in the sexual-abuse cases (and I've met one of them) all appear to be psychopaths.

How did such people get into the seminary after psychological-testing procedures were established? The most notorious cases involved priests who were ordained before testing began. I'm sorry to tell you, I may hold the world's record for testing candidates, having given more than seventeen hundred batteries of psychological tests in thirty years. This is like having the world's largest collection of Royal Crown bottle caps.[7]

Long ago I learned from my excellent teachers at Columbia University that these psychological instruments are helpful to a degree but are not perfect. The accuracy of the results often depends on a person's being honest. If you are testing people for religious life or the priesthood, it may seem fair to assume that they are going to try to be honest. But if they are psychopathic liars, they usually have a choice: they can go to jail or go into politics. And if they don't make it in either one of these, they may try being a clergyman. Sometimes they do all three.

To some extent, America admires psychopaths. P. T. Barnum once said that Americans like humbug, and that's what's happening. In more than one area, American Catholics have been humbugged in the last thirty years. It should be noted that many of the cases now in the papers are about clergy who, perhaps under the influence of alcohol two or three decades ago, engaged in improper actions, but not sexual acts. They went into treatment and have behaved well over the years. Others say that they were misled by the pop psychology of the time — things like Masters and Johnson, or even Kennedy and D'Arcy. They bought into some of the stupid ideas that were floating around in the different denominations at that time, and now they are being destroyed by them.

Some priests who have been removed from public ministerial duties will be back because they are completely innocent, and the only way for them now to clear their names is to put the case into the hands of the civil authorities. Don't assume that every priest taken off the job is guilty. Every priest taken off the job is *accused*. As we know in the case of Joseph Cardinal Bernardin, he was falsely accused. A friend of mine, Archbishop John Ward of Cardiff, Wales, confronted his accuser. It turned out that she made a false charge against the Archbishop at the instigation of people who were furious at the Catholic Church because of its position on abortion.

The Victims and Their Families

What about the victims? They were misled and abused by people who presented themselves as servants of God and His representatives. Many of these victims and their parents chose to remain silent after bringing matters to the attention of Church authorities. It is a great cause of disgust when we hear that the victims were not given adequate attention. I can neither explain nor excuse this neglect. Other victims were given attention by Church authorities and have never made any public accusations. Still others out of the past — perhaps because of bitterness for the scars that they have endured — make large financial demands, perhaps not realizing that the money they are demanding is actually the money of the faithful and not of the clergy.

Will the persecution stop? Sure it will. The media will go off to some other game. They may start on other religious denominations. They may have drifted off to another game even by the time you read this book. They will sail on, but you can be sure right now that they are licking their chops. Once, while I was preaching in the cathedral of a diocese, I denounced a particular newspaper that was viciously anti-Catholic, although it had a largely Catholic readership. After my talk, someone came into the sacristy, and I thought I was going to be laid out. This person said to me, "I was on the editorial staff of that paper for several years, and I want you to know that everything you said about them is true. They sit in the back room and laugh about how they're going to embarrass the Catholic Church." Most of these people have Catholic names.

Where would the immigrants and their children in this country be without the Catholic

Church? Where would they be without Catholic schools and hospitals? My Irish great-grandmother used to say, " 'Tis a sick bird that befouls its own nest."

The Dog That Bites His Own Tail

In the back of medieval cathedrals, there was often a round window that would attract unusual attention. It didn't show a saint or the symbol of a sacrament. It showed a dog biting his own tail. He was twisted around like a doughnut. This dog symbolized the devil. The devil still bites his own tail. If there's any organization in the world that can prove that, it's the Catholic Church. The Church has often buried its undertakers. Sometimes we even give them funerals. You may recall that St. Patrick's Cathedral in New York was attacked a few years ago by a militant, pro-gay group called ACT-UP. They broke up John Cardinal O'Connor's Sunday Mass. They walked around outside the cathedral wearing real religious vestments on which were written obscene words. One of the founders of ACT-UP died of AIDS. And guess who buried him? The Catholic Church.

I'm sure that most of those behind the media blitz — the feeding frenzy against the Catholic Church — have no idea that they are doing the work of Satan. I suspect that the clergy involved in these scandalous acts didn't think they were doing the devil's work, either — although they should have realized it. They may have thought so the next day. I am sure that those who allowed the gay subculture to enter seminaries and religious life and destroy many vocations did not think they were serving Satan, probably because they foolishly did not believe that he exists.

Michael Rose, a conservative Catholic investigative reporter, recently wrote a deeply troubling book about the discouragement of good vocations over the past decade. I know for a fact that much of what Rose says is true, and that good, orthodox, chaste seminarians were discriminated against in some seminaries.[8] Like Rose, I can name names.

The author gives a somewhat lopsided but fairly accurate account of this scandal. It is obvious that the pro-gay agenda of some clergy is directly involved in the Church's present embarrassment and shame. If you are interested in understanding more about the roots of this problem, you would do well to get a copy of Rose's book. We all need to be vigilant because, as it says in the prayer to St. Michael the Archangel, evil spirits "wander through the world, seeking the destruction of souls."

It has often been said that Satan's best defense is to get people to deny his existence. The skepticism that riddles biblical and theological teaching at the present time has caused people to be unaware of the sinister diabolical influence, which was clearly identified by Pope Paul VI.[9] The present crisis, which is rooted in the tradition of theological dissent, is the most obvious example of diabolical influence in our midst. Unfortunately, few can see or acknowledge its presence and action.

This is a time for devout Catholics, other fervent Christians, and all believers in God, like my friends the rabbi and his wife, to turn more fervently to God. It is a time for people to rally against media persecution. There is a terrible lesson to be learned here. As the rabbi's wife said, "What will they do when they turn on us?"

I hope I never again quote Hitler (but you heard the voice of the devil). I could have easily quoted him against Jews, Slavs, Gypsies, black people, and religion in general, but it would always have been the same message: spreading lies in order to destroy.

This particular media blitz of lies is against the Catholic Church. It is not all lies, by any means, but it is a distortion of the truth. According to Jenkins, perhaps at the most, two percent of the clergy in general have been accused in these sexual misbehaviors with young people. Two percent! God help us! That's two percent too many, but it does mean that out of every hundred priests, ninety-eight of them are not involved.

Priests are hurt and demoralized. Many are angry. As I write, it appears that Catholic priests in the United States have no civil rights and are guilty until proved innocent. Any false accusation can remove a priest immediately from his work and home without even the right to confront his accuser or a representative. In fact, the priest may not know the charges. It may take many months for him to be cleared by civil authorities. And in fact, his good name may not be restored. They may simply say that there is insufficient evidence, and his reputation may be ruined. This abuse of the media sets a very dangerous precedent.

Beyond this, there is another deeply objectionable misuse of civil authority. In early May, an assistant district attorney in a county where we are located phoned to ask whether any of our priests had "been reported." Did the assistant district attorney call all the other religious denominations and the large number of independent churches in our area? Is this only a Catholic problem? The media blitz has intimidated the civil and even religious authorities, to the extent that they are suspending basic human rights and throwing equal treatment before the law to the wind. Is this the United States or the Soviet Union? I am well aware that tomorrow I could be removed from my work and deeply embarrassed by a totally false accusation. This is true of every Catholic cleric in the United States.

But there's a flip side that's very interesting. We friars have learned this, and other priests we've talked to have learned it, too. Ever since the media blitz became so intense, more and more people come up to greet us cordially in public. Since we wear our Franciscan habit all the time, they know who we are. I had to leave for England on Easter afternoon while the blitz was at its peak. The young man in charge of the passenger line at the airport kindly put me in first class. When I returned, as I was going through the airport safety precautions, the lady running the X-ray machine wanted her Miraculous Medal blessed. This had never happened before. But it happens often now. The evening before this writing, a priest brought me to a modest Cajun-style restaurant. Not knowing at all who I was, the Ecuadoran waitress kissed me when she saw my Franciscan habit, and the desserts were on the house. Most Americans still have a sense of fairness, and they recognize how unfair the media attack has been.

It is particularly unfair to bishops. Bishops have made mistakes. Some made terrible mistakes. Today's mistakes are not about misbehaving clerics. That's over. Today's mistakes in the Church are about the continuing appointment of people who openly dissent from Church teaching. I will address this in the next chapter. It is a very difficult time to be a bishop. When Bishop Terence Cooke told a friend of his in 1968 that his appointment as Archbishop would be announced in a few hours, he said to his friend, "It's going to be terrible, but that's what '*Fiat Voluntas Tua*' ['Thy Will Be Done'] means."[10] Terence Cardinal Cooke remained loyal to his motto all of the years he was Archbishop.

We who are faithful Catholics need to rally to our Church, and we have to protest when other religions are treated unfairly. Truth is truth, and as time goes on, you will see that the devil will bite his own tail, and that the media will continue to lose more and more credibility in the United States. This will be an unfortunate development because we need the media. Pray. Pray for the Church. Pray for the victims. Pray for our enemies.

It is important for devout Christians to know that they may have to suffer for Jesus Christ. He has suffered for us, St. Peter tells us, and we should rejoice to suffer for him (see Acts 5:41). Right now, Catholics, including the clergy and religious, are very embarrassed. This is part of the price we pay for being Christ's disciples. It is part of the package.

When our little community of friars began, the first sermon I gave them was on this text: "Blessed are you when men revile you and persecute you and utter all kinds of evil against you falsely on my account. Rejoice and be glad, for your reward is great in heaven" (Matthew 5:11-12). Fifteen years later, I would still choose this text.

Endnotes

1. Ronald J. Rychlak, *Hitler, the War, and the Pope* (Huntington, Ind.: Our Sunday Visitor, 2000), p. 94.

2. Ibid., p. 54.

3. Philip Jenkins, "The Myth of the 'Pedophile Priest,' " *Pittsburgh Post-Gazette*, March 3, 2002.

4. Ibid.

5. Bill Keller, "Is the Pope Catholic?" *The New York Times*, May 4, 2002.

6. Maureen Dowd, "The Vatican Rag," *The New York Times*, March 24, 2002.

7. See Benedict J. Groeschel, C.F.R., "Our Priesthood on the Couch," *Crisis*, October 1999.

8. Michael S. Rose, *Goodbye, Good Men* (Washington, D.C.: Regnery Publishing, Inc., 2002).

9. General Audience, November 15, 1972; *L'Osservatore Romano*, November 23, 1972.

10. Benedict J. Groeschel, C.F.R., and Terrence L. Weber, *Thy Will Be Done: A Spiritual Portrait of Terence Cardinal Cooke* (New York: Alba House, 1990), p. 93.

Three

AN URGENT APPEAL FOR REFORM

We now need to ask some questions: What can we do as Catholics and Christians to bring something good out of this terrible scandal and vicious attack on the Church? What can we do to purify the Church in America so that it will live up to its calling to be the voice of Christ in our world? What can we do as individuals to strengthen our leaders so that they will avoid the mistakes, bad judgments, and negligence that have led to this great scandal? It is important to realize that all scandals occur within a historical context. If we do not understand this, as well as the causes of the present scandal, we shall experience what Bishop Sheen called "wasted suffering."

The first thing to keep in mind is that the Gospel calls us to be loyal to Christ and His Church. It will do nothing to rip the Church apart or join in the media frenzy. In the late 1930s, a popular magazine called *Colliers* took a nasty shot at the Catholic Church in an editorial. The Catholics of the United States, from left to right — from Dorothy Day, who was an anarchist, to James Cardinal McIntyre, who was quite conservative — rose as a single person to defend the Church.

Such a response is no longer possible. I have mentioned that on the so-called left, some of the very liberal Catholics are calling for all kinds of changes as a result of this scandal. If these changes were adopted, the Catholic Church would no longer be the Catholic Church, which is perhaps what they would prefer. On the other hand, some very conservative Catholics have foolishly jumped into the feeding frenzy, are joining the enemies of the Church, and are buying into everything being written or said in the media. They really should know better. They have seen how the media unfairly and consistently misrepresent conservative political candidates, and they have pointed this out. Suddenly, they're buying into the whole media package against the Church.

Is there anything the individual can do? Permit me to share the experiences of our little community, the Franciscans of the Renewal. For the last fifteen years, our little communities of friars and sisters of the Renewal have been dedicated to the proposition that the Catholic Church needs reform in the United States and in other English-speaking countries — period! I tried to sum up our position in a book called *The Reform of Renewal* (Ignatius Press, 1990), and I intend to put out a new book on reform as soon as I get the chance — a book called *Reform Now*. In this chapter, I will list some areas I think are pertinent to Church reform, with the understanding that before we do anything else, we must reform ourselves.

The First Step: Reform of Myself
If you were to look through the history of reform, you would find that the most powerful Church reformers often began as individuals — often laypeople — who were trying to bring their own

lives into agreement with the Gospel. They did not set out with the idea of reforming anybody else. St. Francis was very strong on this. He said, "Let everyone judge and despise himself." If you wish to help the Church in this time of grief and shame, it is extremely important to be prepared to look into your own soul and see where you are failing Christ. Don't do this once; do it every day.

Reform is not a depressing experience — quite the opposite. It is very healthy at the end of the day to kneel down and look at your shortcomings, at the sins you've committed with half-attention and distraction, and to assess your own mediocrity. It can also be very helpful to recite Psalm 51 before going to sleep:

> Have mercy on me, O God,
>   according to thy steadfast love;
>   according to thy abundant mercy blot out
>   my transgressions. . . .
>
> Hide thy face from my sins,
>   and blot out all my iniquities.
>
> Create in me a clean heart, O God,
>   and put a new and right spirit within me.
> Cast me not away from thy presence,
>   and take not thy holy Spirit from me.

Restore to me the joy of thy salvation
and uphold me with a willing spirit.

Then I will teach transgressors thy ways,
and sinners will return to thee. . . .

The sacrifice acceptable to God is a broken
spirit,
a broken and contrite heart, O God, thou
wilt not despise. (Psalm 51:1-2, 9-13, 17)

Unfortunately, the spirit of repentance and contrition is rather rare in the English-speaking world right now. This is due in part to the uncritical acceptance of psychological theories based on self-esteem, self-expression, self-importance, and self-fulfillment. In the catastrophe that has come upon the Church, the lack of wisdom in applying these theories is all too apparent. People were told to "do your thing" so that they might be healthy. We should be doing the things of God. People were given the impression that psychotherapy could somehow make them good. Like all other things, therapy can help, but we are saved by Christ alone. To rely completely on any process of human origin for mental and spiritual health is Pelagianism, a heresy that has been around for sixteen hundred years.

Reform and the Laity

Many reformers in Church history were laypeople, either when they started or all through their lives. St. Catherine of Siena was always a laywoman. So was St. Catherine of Genoa. St. Francis of Assisi and St. Ignatius Loyola both started out as laymen without any idea of starting a community.

St. Catherine of Genoa (1447–1510) lived in a time of renewal: new architecture, new music, and new ways of doing things.[1] She made it clear that renewal without reform would kill the Church. She lived during the Renaissance, on the eve of the Protestant Reformation and the worldly renewal led by such popes as Alexander VI and Leo X. This renewal almost did kill the Church. She busied herself with the care of the sick and poor — and with founding prayer groups, the first ones in history in which the clergy and laity gathered to read the Scriptures and pray. Historians credit Catherine with beginning the Catholic Reformation.[2]

Reform is not a vague idea. When we turn our eyes from ourselves and look at the situation around us, we realize that we must have some very specific ideas on what needs to be reformed. It would be all too easy simply to say that those clergy involved in sexual misbehavior must be dismissed or at least put into a penitential situation where they can change. Those who have been involved in endangering minors obviously have to be effectively removed from all contact with youngsters.

But the sexual scandals of the present moment are unfortunately only the symptom of the disease. The disease goes much deeper. Practically all serious Catholics who look at the symptoms I list will know that we have been part of the problem, even when we didn't mean to be. Now we are looking for people to be part of the solution. As the saying goes, if you're not part of the solution, then you are part of the problem.

What Can I Do?

A layperson, parish priest, or religious brother or sister may ask, "What can I do?" You can lead your life in an appropriate way, following the Gospel, no matter what anyone else says. To do this, the prayerful daily reading of the Gospel and the New Testament, and even of the whole Bible, can be a wonderful guide. We have allowed the skepticism of some scholars to cause us to read the Bible with little interest, with diffidence, and even with skepticism. Read the Scriptures as the word of God and not as the words of men.

Another area needing serious attention is the reception of the sacraments, particularly the Sacraments of Reconciliation and the Holy Eucharist. Before we even begin to think about reform, we have to ask ourselves this question: "Do I pray fervently with an open heart and keen desire when I receive the Eucharist and when I prepare myself for the Sacrament of Reconciliation?" These are not idle, pious thoughts. Check and see if you are part of mediocre Catholicism, even if you work full-time for the Church as a priest, religious, or layperson.

Having said this, let's look at some of the areas that obviously need reform. I do not have time in this book to go into these extensively; consequently, my remarks must be generalized and to the point.

Liturgy and Public Prayer

In the past thirty years, there has been a seemingly endless amount of talk about liturgy and changes in liturgy, about the comings and goings in liturgy. When all is said and done, the public prayer of the Church is often shabby, distracting, and confusing to non-Catholics who come to visit our services. The behavior of a Catholic congregation does not match up favorably with that of a

Protestant or Jewish congregation, which you will find out if you occasionally visit another group of believers when they are praying. Catholics, including the clergy at times, act as if prayer is just an obligation to be disposed of as quickly as possible. Supposedly, the post-Vatican II era was to have been a time of liturgical renewal. Endless numbers of stories circulate among the clergy and laity about silly attempts at renewal, bringing things into the liturgy that were distracting and did not focus our attention on the presence of Christ and the representation of His holy life, death, and resurrection.

If you want to do something about the public prayer of the Church, go to church decently dressed, to begin with. Liturgy has become so casual — even Sunday Mass — that people do not even dress properly. The one exception is the poor. We friars are so blessed because we work with the poor. The poor never go to church badly dressed. You couldn't force them with a gun to enter a church badly dressed. But in middle-class parishes on Sunday morning, people look as if they're going to the beach. And in upper-class parishes, they often look as if they're coming back from the beach.

The worship of God is something serious. It does not require formal attire, but it certainly deserves dignified and appropriate attire. Moreover, our whole appearance should reflect that we are engaged in something very serious. People might ask themselves, "Would I go see the doctor, dressed as I am going to church?"

Along with being properly attired, it is certainly appropriate for people attending Mass to be both dignified and thoughtful of others. Not so long ago, no one spoke aloud in a Catholic church. Unfortunately, there now seems to be open conversation before and after Mass, with very little, if any, attention paid to those who would like to be recollected and pray before Mass begins or when Mass ends. If you want to do something to begin Church reform, start by asking others around you to please be quiet so you can pray. And always avoid talking aloud in church. I notice that people do not mind and are perhaps impressed when I ask them to speak to me after Mass and outside the church.

Prayer at Mass and other church services should always be devout and should focus on the great sacrament of Christ's Sacrifice and Presence. I have written extensively about this in my book *In the Presence of Our Lord* (Our Sunday Visitor, 1997), where you will see listed some of the most horrific examples of dissident thinking and absurd ideas about the liturgy and the Eucharist. It is no accident that there is a lack of respect for the presence of Christ in the Eucharist. Often the care and custody of the Eucharist approaches the scandalous, even the sacrilegious.

Obviously, there are different liturgical approaches for different congregations of people. Older people like me prefer something sedate and prayerful. Teenagers will be moved by something quite different. Whatever we do, it should be prayerful. And what is prayer? It is the lifting of the mind and heart to God, not to one another. It is not a lifting up to us ourselves. The liturgy is not a performance, and it is not meant to be entertainment. You can and should support the best liturgy in your parish, and you should ask for it.

It seems that everybody has an idea of what liturgy should be. Sometimes parish liturgy committees are made up of people who have never read one word of liturgical theology or any of the Church's authoritative directives on the Mass or liturgy. Some wouldn't know how to spell the word "liturgy." But whatever it is, the liturgy should be prayerful, dignified, and move the heart and soul. It should follow the missal and liturgical norms. There is a very special room in purgatory for clergy who make up their own liturgy, and it ain't nice there.

A significant element of prayer is *devotion*. This word has been belittled in seminaries for so long that many young men now seeking to be priests don't know what it means. Devotion is a vibrant psychological conviction that Christ in eternal glory, the heavenly Father, the Holy Spirit, Our Lady, or one of the saints knows me. It is the realization that in some divine way God is aware of me, or that in some spiritual way, with God's help, Our Lady or a saint is aware of me.

God cares for me. He listens to my prayer for those I love and care about, and for the whole world. He also expects things of me, and when I fail, He requires me to be penitent. God also expects me to do His will and accept what life may bring, to depend on His grace to get me through and bring some good out of evil. This is especially true when we turn in devotion to Christ crucified and suffering. Although He suffered long ago, the memory of His suffering, which has strengthened armies of saints, would make a great deal of sense when we are trying to pray in times of need, failure, or desperation.

While we are talking about devotion, we might say that every Catholic has the right to go to a church that looks like a Catholic church. We are not Quakers. I expect Quakers to go to Quaker meetinghouses, which are meant to be very plain and white, according to the teachings of the Society of Friends. This is not part of the Catholic tradition at all. It never was. We should have in our churches objects of art and edification, which lift our minds and hearts to God. The greatest religious art in the history of the world is in the possession of the Catholic Church. Some reflection of that should be found even in our humblest chapels.

Catholic Education

The principal problem in Catholic education at the present time, from kindergarten to university, is that it is undermined by a spirit of dissent. This spirit has actually existed since before the Second Vatican Council, and it has caused a great deal of confusion. People teaching Catholic religious doctrine are allowed to decide for themselves when and how to dissent. There is even a psychological habit of dissent on the part of some religious and priests, so that if they are not dissenting, they seem to feel guilty. Many's the priest, religious, or layperson who has suffered disdain, rejection, or ridicule for refusing to countenance dissent. This filters down through college, high school, and elementary school. How many Catholic parents are deeply disappointed that they spent their hard-earned money to send their children to a Catholic college, or even a Catholic high school, where the children were taught things that are inimical to the Catholic faith and morals? In such schools, children pick up not only a spirit of dissent but also a spirit of disrespect and irreligion.

This problem has to be looked at seriously in order to get to the root of the larger problem. In a series of very enlightening articles, George Weigel, the distinguished Catholic writer and biographer of the Pope, has summed up the problem in Catholic education. Weigel maintains that in today's confused culture "any religious institution that does not self-consciously, deliberately, and unceasingly work to maintain its orthodoxy will inevitably become corrupted, doctrinally and behaviorally."[3] "Orthodoxy" means the fullness of teaching. It's a very good word, although in some Catholic quarters it has taken on a bad meaning.

When orthodoxy is not embraced and there is a psychological proclivity toward disagreeing with orthodoxy, the result is a culture of dissent. Weigel gives an excellent description of this:

> A culture of dissent has been a staple feature of Catholic life — sometimes blatantly overt, sometimes less obvious — since the birth

control controversy of 1968. In recent years the culture of dissent has been more subtle, as reforms of seminaries and diocesan offices have been undertaken with some success. But the habit of dissent has been hard to break. Indeed, one of the stranger features of contemporary Catholicism in America is the branding of self-consciously orthodox younger clergy and scholars as "ideologues" who are to be consigned to the margins of church life.[4]

Weigel defends the noticeable emerging group of young people — especially young priests, seminarians, and even some young religious — who wish to be loyal to the Church and its teachings in a wholehearted way. Despite the inadequate religious education and training these young people have often received, they are practically a theological miracle. To me, they are the greatest single sign that the Church will recover from the present disaster; however, it must be said that they would not be there if it were not for the Holy Spirit.

The culture of dissent is most obvious in Catholic colleges and universities. There are religion courses that are very far from anything resembling Catholic teaching or the communication of the Gospel. Often, there are teachers who are notoriously and viciously hostile to the Pope and to the teaching Magisterium of the Church. It is not my intent to go into this at length here, but it could be documented extensively. And I intend to document it when I write my next book, *Reform Now*.

One example comes to mind. At a recent national meeting of Catholic college presidents, a professor of philosophy from a Jesuit university was given the opportunity to make a presentation. He identified himself as an atheist and was filled with self-congratulation that a Catholic college could have an atheist teaching philosophy. Believe me, he is not the only atheist teaching philosophy in a Catholic college.

The Catholic colleges and universities of the United States were built by poor, immigrant people, as well as by Catholics who had managed to be a bit more successful. They were built as part of the educational apostolate of the Catholic Church, and their buildings were part of Catholic Church property, usually in the hands of religious communities, which are under the jurisdiction of the Pope himself. These facilities have been alienated from the Catholic Church in a most unjust violation of the will of the benefactors. On so many occasions, these facilities are used not to lead people to Christ, which was the intention of their builders, but to make people even more worldly and dissident.

If I were to cite more examples of this, it would be difficult to know where to begin. I would rather say that there is a small group of loyal Catholic colleges and an even smaller group of loyal Catholic universities. Some smaller Catholic colleges in the hands of religious communities are beginning to find their way back. If I had a family of my own, I must admit I would be very hard-pressed to name more than twenty Catholic colleges in the United States where I would be willing to send my child.

My observation is neither idle nor uninformed. I am on the board of directors of two Catholic institutions of higher learning, Franciscan University and Ave Maria College, and I have been teaching seminarians for almost forty years. I have also taught in Catholic colleges and universities on the graduate level as an adjunct professor. When I left these institutions, it was most often because I did not want to participate in something that was really not representative of or in any substantial agreement with the teachings of the Catholic Church specifically, or even of Christianity generally.

Is there anything that an individual Catholic can do? First of all, most of my readers will be alumni of Catholic colleges or high schools. Find out what's going on. If they write to you for money, make sure you know what they are up to. The egregious abuse of Catholic education is so bad right now that it would not be difficult to find the scandal of dissent if it is there. You might only have to visit the campus and look at the bulletin boards. Visit the chapel and see what is going on.

If you are inclined to donate to Catholic education, be sure to donate to what is genuinely and loyally Catholic. Many institutions are now violating the commandments. For many institutions to call themselves Catholic is indeed a violation of the Second Commandment; they take the name of the Lord in vain.

Most of my readers will be more likely to have some influence in Catholic primary or secondary education or in religious education. If you are a parent or in some other way responsible for children's education, you have every right to look at the textbooks and the content of the religious education your children are receiving. This is particularly true if you are paying tuition in a high school or an elementary school. Even in secular education, things are often done over the heads of the parents. Egregious mistakes have been made not only in areas like sex education (which should really be education in chastity), but also in the straightforward presentation of Catholic doctrine. All parents have the right and duty to see that their children are educated by those who accept and support the Church's moral teachings. The time is over for parents to be dismissed in a patronizing way when they have legitimate objections. Some of those who are conducting religious education today are themselves only lukewarm Catholics, and perhaps not even observant Catholics, while others who are teaching espouse the culture of dissent. Throughout the English-speaking world, there are informed parents who have been doing their own religious educating. While this approach may help them and their children, it does take the pressure off the whole system to provide good religious education.

The Root of the Problem

We might well ask: What in the world is the root of all of this culture of dissent? Where did it come from, since Catholic life was vibrant until the time of Vatican II? It is my conviction that it did not come from the Council; in fact, the Council, if anything, was a providential pressure valve that kept the damage from becoming even worse.

In Europe, and gradually in the United States, skepticism about religious belief became rampant in the liberal Protestant world and then in the Catholic world. Much of this skepticism at first focused on the teaching and understanding of Sacred Scripture, or the Bible. While the people involved were well-intentioned and most scholarly, they allowed themselves to be drawn into very skeptical positions. Well-meaning and well-educated teachers would tell the faithful that Jesus did not know who He was, and other similar things. There was an ignoring of the immense mysteries of our faith: the Incarnation, the divine knowledge, the divine person of Jesus Christ, His extraordinary human knowledge, as well as the fact that He was free from the effects of original sin, especially the darkening of the intellect. These truths were not only ignored but also reduced to the simple, flat declarative statement that Jesus did not know who He was. When you stand back and look at such a denial, it is difficult to imagine that a person could have retained his faith and still thought such a thing. In fact, the idea that Jesus did not know when the last day would occur at the end of the world was condemned by Pope St. Gregory the Great fourteen hundred years ago.[5]

Many other skeptical ideas came into play, which made it almost impossible for the docile seminarian to preach the Scriptures when he became a priest. Did Jesus really multiply the loaves and fish? Did He really speak to the wind and the sea? Was His mother really a virgin? Did He physically rise from the dead? These questions may sound horrible to you, but I know people studying theology and religious education who have been told things like the following quotation, which was uttered by a woman who teaches laity to be pastoral assistants in a diocesan program: "Nobody believes anymore that Jesus really, physically rose from the dead." Oh, yeah?

A friend of mine attending a doctoral program in theology with an emphasis on Sacred Scripture at a respected Catholic university recently told me that the entire procedure was without any soul. It was simply a series of intellectual discussions, complex ideas, and ancient readings, but there was absolutely no personal conviction or heart in the whole thing at all.

The people involved in all this are, I'm sure, sincere people. They are fulfilling what they think is their vocation. But how is it that they could teach the Scriptures, which are a double-edged sword reaching into our hearts and minds? The study of Sacred Scripture is intended to bring alive in us not only the words of God but also His will and the earnest appeal of Christ for us to follow

Him. What we have now is a rather disengaged, academic tradition filled with the culture of dissent, without any real application of Sacred Scripture to individual lives. I would happily debate anyone in public on this statement. Thankfully, there are exceptions — a growing number of exceptions — but the overall picture in the teaching of Sacred Scripture is that it is academic, intellectualized, remote, lifeless, and filled with skepticism.

Unfortunately, for decades seminarians and college students have been treated almost exclusively to a particular approach associated with the historical-critical method of Scripture scholarship. This method had its origins in nineteenth-century German skepticism and still carries much of that burden. We constantly hear that this scientific method justifies our saying that Jesus did not work this miracle or that miracle, or that He did not know who He was.

Indeed, first of all, this is absolutely unscientific. The last thing you would ever do in science is to prove that something *didn't* happen. That is called a negative hypothesis, and in scientific investigation it is avoided. Second, many theories that are presented as "gospel truth" are, in fact, scientifically most improbable. They are based on strings of possibilities, one after the other, which reduce their probability to such a small figure that it is almost impossible to calculate it numerically. Nonetheless, laity and religious are told that these are certain and true.

The simple fact is that we have the Scriptures given to us by Divine Providence to guide us to salvation. The Church has declared that they are the work of the Holy Spirit and also inerrant. If you wonder why Sunday sermons are vague, it is because the person preaching has been prepared, not to preach the Gospel, but rather to critique it — something he is usually totally unprepared to do — and perhaps even to critique it in ways that no one should attempt.

My complaint about the teaching of Sacred Scripture being remote and lifeless can also be made about the teaching of systematic or dogmatic theology. Theology is supposed to teach us to know and love God and the things of God. If it is taught in a wholly abstract way without reference to individual spiritual needs, it will become an obstacle to faith rather than a help to faith. The dull, abstract teaching of theology is, of course, nothing new. It has happened throughout the centuries. But having studied theology under very dull conditions years ago, I can at least say it gave me plenty to pray and think about. Now it is so abstract and frequently filled with dissent, or at least uncertainty, that if one were to pray about it, it might be better to ask to be delivered from it.

Another area of teaching that has become very confused is moral theology, or the teaching of morality. This was always strong and clear in the Catholic Church up until about the 1960s, but then it began to be vague. It goes beyond the scope of this book to present the various opinions that have made sin almost disappear. Many people complain that it is difficult to go to confession because confessions are not heard. The root of the problem is that virtue and sin are not preached. Our divine Savior in the Gospels, especially in the parables and in the Sermon on the Mount, clearly indicates His very real moral expectations of those who would be His disciples. One of the outstanding Scripture scholars of modern times, Father Rudolf Schnackenburg, makes it eminently clear that the founder of Christianity had very high expectations of those who would follow Him. At the same time, He was merciful and forgiving. But once people returned to Him, He would expect more and more of them.[6]

The widespread failure to teach sexual morality has done considerable harm to the Church. Voluntary sexual behavior outside marriage is forbidden by the Gospel and the Christian tradition. Sexual behavior in marriage is legitimate only when there is no artificial contraception of one kind or another. Both of these teachings can be difficult to observe. Today, however, people are not being taught about divine mercy and the limitations of their freedom; instead the Church's teaching about what is right and wrong is being watered down. This has created an immense amount of moral confusion and has made the moral behavior of Catholics almost indistinguishable from the behavior of people who have few or no religious values at all.

Later we will say more about the pro-life movement and the necessity of supporting life, but even the Church's teaching against abortion is often poorly presented. Catholic public officials who are known to support abortion gravely damage their own conscience and give open scandal, yet they continue to receive support, accolades, and embraces from representatives of the Church. This represents, among other things, a lack of charity, even to those politicians, because they should be reminded that by supporting abortion, they have called their own eternal salvation into the gravest question. How is it that we Catholics have gone along with so much?

When we consider all of this and try to take into account the various examples of clerical sexual misbehavior with minors, it seems obviously to be all of a piece. These priests have convinced themselves or been convinced by others that certain sexual sins are not sinful. Anyone who knows anything about temptation and sin knows that a conflicted person will be "drawn over Niagara Falls." Sexual sin is like that. It is infectious and grips a person like an octopus. St. Augustine, writing about sexual sin and his battle to give it up, said, "What held me was so small a thing, but it held me nonetheless . . . and I feared that that thin, frail tie would grow strong again and bind me even closer than before."[7]

Is it surprising, then, that on the part of some of the clergy there has been a failure to observe their own promises of chastity and celibacy, and to uphold the teachings of the Church?

Religious-Order Priests

It is the duty of a parish priest not to break the bruised reed or quench the smoking flax (see Isaiah 42:3). This means that when he teaches the hard sayings, he has to teach them with understanding and gentleness, but he still has to teach them.

I think that priests who are members of religious orders and who are not assigned to parishes have a much more serious obligation to identify what is sinful and what goes against the Gospel. By both their religious profession and their priesthood, they are bound to uphold the teachings of the Catholic Church. By reason of their religious vocation and the fact that they do not serve in parishes, they are, of all Christians except bishops, the most responsible for upholding and teaching the moral law.

There are many sad examples in America today of religious-order priests who do precisely the opposite, particularly those engaged in education. If the Catholic Church in the United States is to recover its dignity as well as the respect of its own members and that of our fellow citizens, we must begin to practice what we preach. There is no other way. Individuals, groups of clergy, and religious teachers all need to undertake a thoroughgoing, overall examination of conscience; those who are unwilling or unable to do this should drop out of teaching. It could very well happen that the impatience of the Catholic community with any more moral nonsense will force them to this position.

Seminary Training

It is no secret in the Catholic community that the quality of seminary training is very uneven.

The faithful attending Sunday Mass are well aware of this themselves. Experiences range from young priests who are well-prepared to those who simply don't know what they're talking about and have not received the knowledge necessary for pastoral care. There has been a tendency on the part of some seminaries to train priests to be "pastoral ministers" rather than preachers of the Gospel and priests of the Church. Those attending Mass can get the impression that they are in a group-therapy session or at a pep rally rather than hearing a homily on Sacred Scripture guided by the teaching of the Church. I know a number of young priests who have gone to institutes and training programs at their own expense to make up for the theological deficiencies of their seminary training.

The subject is so large that one hesitates to take it up. However, having taught in seminaries for almost forty years and having been thrown out or eased out of at least three, I think I speak with a certain amount of experience. Several negative influences entered seminary life after the Second Vatican Council.

The first was theological relativism based on skepticism. Skepticism identical with the skepticism we spoke of in biblical studies is not a body of teachings but rather an attitude of mind that often arises from a misapplication of scientific procedures to subjects like theology and Scripture. Ultimately, these procedures, which we refer to as scientific, do not apply to such disciplines, which deal with transcendent mysteries. Science is about the measurable. Theology and Scripture are about the immeasurable.

In science, there is a principle called "minimalism," according to which if you cannot understand or deal with something, you ultimately put it on the side; if you are a foolish scientist, you may even pretend that it does not exist. Actually, a good scientist would not do that. He would simply file away the unknowable and incomprehensible phenomenon until later, when he might try to fit it into his theoretical structure.

Unfortunately, as has often happened since the late Middle Ages, the wedding of scientific procedures and theological discourse resulted in a muddled union. This goes back to the time of William of Ockham, an excommunicated Franciscan who is famous in people's minds for what is called "Ockham's razor" — that is, the practice of cutting away what is difficult or incomprehensible.

Minimalism joins forces almost immediately with skepticism, or an attitude of unbelief. In the last forty years, I have read books and heard lectures by people assigned to teach theology, Scripture, or philosophy, and I did not know why they still identified themselves as Christians. I did not doubt the sincerity of their statements but questioned the plausibility of their finding themselves in the Christian faith, which requires acceptance of mysteries that are inscrutable and unfathomable.

What many seminarians were fed was an approach to Scripture and theology that grew more and more skeptical. Being young and impressionable, they would react in one of two ways: either they would embrace the skepticism and become very lax in their moral and prayer life, as well as in their intellectual approach to things, or they would become defensive and at times fundamentalistic, reducing divine mysteries to the level of their own thoughts, which they could comprehend. At least those moving toward fundamentalism would retain their faith, although they would become vulnerable. Since seminarians for the most part are young men, they were not prepared for the essential step of the spiritual life in which mature faith expresses itself by the acceptance of divine mystery. Albert Einstein had this to say about his approach to mystery: "The fairest thing we can experience is the mysterious. It is the fundamental emotion which stands at the cradle of true art and science. . . . A knowledge of the existence of something we cannot penetrate, of the manifestations of the profoundest reason and the most radiant beauty, which are only accessible to our reason in their most elementary forms — it is this knowledge and this emotion that constitute the truly religious attitude." At least those who moved toward a more fundamentalist approach retained the ability later on to retrieve and reevaluate things in the sense of a more mature faith.

Many of my readers have heard sermons that called into serious question basic dogmas of the Catholic faith. This was often done in the most superficial — and one may say asinine — way. There is the account of a young priest who pointed to the Eucharist one Sunday morning and said, "This is not the Body of Christ. We are the Body of Christ." Eighty percent of the people in the church froze. Twenty percent had their wits about them and got up and left. They immediately appealed to the pastor, who said that he couldn't do anything; so they went to the bishop. The bishop also said he could do nothing, so nothing happened. This kind of theological erosion is gravely, morally deficient on all sides. Not only were the people in the church the victims, but the young priest was also a victim of scandalously shoddy education. He was really giving the people a teaching of Huldrych Zwingli, founder of the Reformed Church.

After the Council, there was an honest effort to make theology more interesting. The mistake, however, was trying to make it more relevant — that is, more agreeable to a society that was moving toward paganism. A sorry example of a book that took a lot of work but fell into the double trap of dissent and disguised secular humanism is *Catholicism*, by Father Richard McBrien. Anyone familiar with this book will see that it reflects the very attitudes that Cardinal Newman had identified and warned about in his great work *The Idea of a University*. In that sense, I contrast Father McBrien and many other contemporary writers of theology with John Paul II. The Pope writes with beauty and power. What do the self-styled American progressive Catholics writers mean, and where are they going? The following quotation from Newman seems almost prophetic:

> Truth has two attributes — beauty and power. . . . Pursue it, either as beauty or power, to its furthest extent and its true limit, and you

are led by either road to the Eternal and Infinite, to the intimations of conscience and the announcements of the Church. Satisfy yourself with what is only visibly or intelligibly excellent, as you are likely to do, and you will make present utility and natural beauty the practical test of truth, and the sufficient object of the intellect. It is not that you will at once reject Catholicism, but you will measure and proportion it by an earthly standard. You will throw its highest and most momentous disclosures into the background, you will deny its principles, explain away its doctrines, re-arrange its precepts, and make light of its practices, even while you profess it. Knowledge, viewed as knowledge, exerts a subtle influence in throwing us back on ourselves, and making us our own centre, and our own minds the measure of all things. This is [its] tendency . . . to view Revealed Religion from an aspect of its own — to fuse and recast it — to tune it, as it were, to a different key, and to reset its harmonies, to circumscribe it by a circle which unwarrantably amputates here, and unduly develops there; and all under the notion, conscious or unconscious, that the human intellect, self-educated and self-supported, is more true and perfect in its ideas and judgments than that of Prophets and Apostles, to whom the sights and sounds of Heaven were immediately conveyed. . . .

Let this spirit be freely evolved out of . . . [a] philosophical condition of mind . . . and it is impossible but, first indifference, then laxity of belief, then even heresy will be the successive results.[8]

I cannot go completely into the matter of seminary training here, except to say that it desperately needs reform. In fact, in the last several years, reform seems to be under way in many places because younger priests who were educated long after the confusing time following Vatican II are returning to teach and seem to have their feet on the ground. Many of these young priests themselves will complain bitterly about their experiences as seminarians. A word of defense might be said of their teachers. I do not question that the teachers in the 1970s and 1980s had goodwill and thought that they were doing their best. I was one of them, and I made mistakes, too. I do, at times, question their orthodoxy as well as their common sense. I have seen too many things that were not only heretical, or bordering on heresy, but also simply absurd and preposterous.

The Gay Scene

Perhaps the most sinister element entering into seminary life was the so-called gay scene. A permissive attitude toward homosexual mannerisms and even behavior was observable in varying degrees in a number of seminaries. To some degree, this is not surprising, because the same was true in all higher education. Blatant encouragement of sexual deviation was observable in almost every secular college and university in the United States, with large militant gay organizations making a good deal of noise. One has to recall that all this gay agitation to change public attitudes toward homosexuals and homosexuality was successfully accomplished despite the findings of serious polltakers who maintain that there is a steady rate of adult men who claim to be homosexual at less than three percent. Never before in the history of the world have less than three percent made so much of an impact on ninety-seven percent.

Gradually, as some seminaries lost their way, the gay culture entered in. In a number of seminaries, it was simply not tolerated at all; in others, it achieved a subtle acceptance and approval by keeping a low profile, but people knew it was there. Finally, in some seminaries it became scandalously

apparent, and those who opposed it were casti-
gated as intolerant and puritanical.

A sad and shocking but comprehensive survey of this phenomenon can be found in Michael
Rose's book *Goodbye, Good Men*, which we mentioned in the last chapter. Although Rose is writing advocacy literature and at times overstates his
case, the facts are there. As may happen in such
literature, he may move over the line occasionally into gossip or an overly judgmental attitude
toward those who are trying to walk a middle way.
However, any honest person reading Rose's book
will admit that he gives facts, figures, and direct
testimony of people by name. I know some of the
people he mentions, and I also know of the injustices and suffering they endured because they were
considered intolerant of the gay scene. I know very
well because I endured the same injustices for the
same reason.

It is important to make the following distinction when discussing this complex problem. On
the one hand, we must be accepting of a person
who struggles with any kind of problem, including a sexual problem. On the other hand, we must
state clearly that sexual misbehavior of any kind
does not belong in the lives of those who present
themselves before the world as Christ's disciples,

especially those who perform His sacred ministries. The catastrophic situation in the Catholic Church in the United States right now needs to be honestly placed where it belongs. It is not pedophilia. It is homosexuality.

Often associated with homosexual identity are types of behavior that can be classified as "campy," or effeminate in a negative sense. This kind of behavior on the part of someone vowed to priestly celibacy or aspiring to it is directly scandalous and utterly uncalled for. I have worked for much of my life with homosexually oriented people struggling and succeeding at leading chaste lives. Even if they should have some unduly effeminate characteristics (or masculine ones, if they are women), these devout people do not belong to the gay scene and often lead lives of great religious fervor and chastity. This is what we find in the excellent organization called Courage. Others are not yet leading a chaste life, but they go to church and at least they are not recruiting people for the gay scene. They may well convert to chastity in the future.[9]

The problems with seminaries are generally known to the members of the Catholic community. Some seminarians don't ask too many questions, because they are told to mind their own business. They don't say very much, because they don't know too much. It is therefore incumbent on ex-seminarians who suffered injustices and ordained priests who are basically safe in their vocation to speak up about these problems. Every diocesan bishop or religious superior who has a seminary program under his care must face his grave responsibility to see that those who are ordained have been well prepared in chastity and can take care of the Catholic people without scandal.

As someone who has taught in good seminaries and bad, I must say that next to pedophilia itself and the sexual abuse of young people, the negligence and poor performance of some seminaries is the most disturbing part of the present scandalous situation in which Catholics find themselves. I also believe that an immediate reform of seminaries that are off the track would lead to an increase of vocations and a restoration of confidence on the part of the faithful. Rose's hypothesis is that the corruption of seminaries was purposeful in order to undermine the celibate male priesthood. I am not sure if I would go that far. However, I do know a woman religious, who taught at and dominated a seminary for a number of years, who directly told a reliable priest-friend of mine that "the sooner the Catholic Church gets rid of celibate priests and religious, the better off everybody will be." Anyone wishing to hold such an opinion in a free country is at liberty to do so. But it violates the intentions of those who financially support a seminary if an influential person in that program directly opposes its purposes, goals, and even inspiration. Church reform must include the reform of seminary training where it is needed. And all that has been said applies as well to adult educational and pastoral programs for laity.

Religious Life

For older Catholics, one of the saddest aspects of life in the last thirty years has been the destruction of religious orders. Nobody wants to use the word "destruction," but that is exactly what has happened. It is necessary to approach this painful topic with care because a great many people who were responsible for this destruction proceeded on goodwill but with an incredible naïveté. Religious communities have naïvely taken direction from people in the behavioral sciences who do not even believe in God, much less in Christian revelation. The communities have ignored almost entirely the example and teaching of their founders and the consistent instructions of the Holy See, and of the popes in particular, on the necessary components of religious life. One could excuse the religious of the past for at times being naïve, since they lived in a world somewhat removed from human weakness and wickedness. That cannot be said anymore, because most religious have moved into secularized situations, where they should be able to perceive the obvious results of the worldly and un-Christian understanding of human existence.

Putting it very bluntly, religious stand before the world as those who have professed in the name of Christ to follow poverty, chastity, and obedience. These are the essential components of religious life observed even by non-Christian religious, like Buddhists and Hindus. When these components are absent or are present only in a superficial, ritualistic way, religious life is going to decline. It is in catastrophic decline at the present time.

One would need the utmost gifts of imagination to call the existence of many religious "religious life." Any number of religious who live on their own and make their way painfully in the world lament the loss of religious life. This is particularly true of religious sisters. They want to be religious, but their communities no longer provide any real opportunity for this.

Probably the worst mistake that was made was to give up religious garb. Victor Turner, the outstanding psychological anthropologist, in his study of liminal groups — that is, groups that stand outside of society — points out that a plain, identifiable, uniform religious garb is an essential component of this kind of life.[10] According to Turner, you can't be a nun or a hippie unless you look like one, because these are liminal, or outsider, groups. At times during history, persecution has forced some groups of religious not to wear identifiable garb or even to be known as religious, but religious garb has generally been accepted as an essential component of religious life for well over fifteen hundred years. Where are the communities now who gave up this garb?

Apart from that, many communities have jettisoned even more essential things traditionally considered components of religious life: some form of real community life; the observance of poverty, or at least frugality; the common ownership of goods; and the strict observance of chastity. When religious failed in any of these in the past, it was the tradition to repent deeply, confess their sins, and if they had given public scandal, acknowledge this before the community and perhaps even before others.

The changes that have been made in religious life in the last forty years have led to catastrophe.

The great religious communities of sisters that taught millions of Catholics in the past with great success are now in the final stages of disintegration. Newer communities, and a few intrepid examples of older communities that held on to their identity, are leading the way. They are, to use the popular expression, "getting vocations." The others are simply drying up. A few communities have put a foot in both camps, although they have stood admirably against the tide. They wonder why they're not getting vocations. It may well be that their efforts are good, but not good enough to attract the very earnest and sincere young people who are looking for the challenge of religious life at the present time. A number of new religious communities have started, and they frequently find that they are able to attract at least enough vocations to make a serious impact on mainstream Church life.

Reform is absolutely necessary in religious life now. I can do little more here than simply state the fact. Religious who want to do something in the way of reform but who belong to orders that have lost their way and identity should first go away and make a long, silent, private retreat. This was the very experience that led to reform of religious life in the seventeenth century. Don't go looking for suggestions, plans, and roundtable discussions. All religious worthy of their name should quietly go before the Eucharist and ask our Divine Savior to renew their vocation and lead them away from any worldliness, laxity, skepticism, or unbelief that has entered their lives. As long as, and wherever, the Church has existed, religious life has been there. It will not be destroyed, but it must be renewed. Those who join the renewal will find that their lives will have meaning; those who do not join it will find that their lives will be sorrowfully frustrated or, much worse, will lead to something that will endanger their own salvation.

The Priesthood

For the past several months, the Catholic priesthood has been exposed to the most bitter media attacks. Tragically, they were aimed at the institution of the priesthood as a whole, but for only a relatively small number of priests did the attacks have any basis in reality. Some priests have been guilty of serious misbehavior, whether in the distant past or the recent past. Sometimes, as we have said, they were guilty of severe moral lapses that caused great harm to others; sometimes they committed lesser indiscretions that are now being seen in a very nasty light.

All of this, of course, causes us to focus some attention on the priesthood. I have been a priest for forty-three years. It has been a time of joy and intense hard work, and my greatest problem as a priest has been to find the time to do everything I could do. I have had the greatest fulfillment in pastoral service to all kinds of people, but especially those in difficulties and in trouble, starting with the youngsters at Children's Village and later working with priests in their spiritual journey for thirty years. During these times, I have enjoyed the friendship of clergy of other religious denominations, both Christian and Jewish. I have also been blessed to know non-Catholic women clergy, who face the same challenges as all other clergy and perhaps a few more as well. The care of souls has been a wonderful joy to me.

I have known priests who are likely to be formally canonized as saints, and I have known others who left the priesthood in disgrace, which they brought on themselves or at least collaborated with. At times, I wondered if they had been directly drawn into these things by diabolical influences.

With all of this, and after having given at least five hundred retreats to priests over the last thirty years, I can say with no hesitation that the Catholic priesthood urgently needs a renewal of the spiritual life. This is not to imply that priests are not interested in their spiritual lives; many are. But in the United States, the vast majority of priests at present, especially those in parish and pastoral work, are immensely overburdened and facing impossible tasks. The spiritual life then begins to look like a luxury — something one cannot afford to have. The very priests who tell me they don't have anyone to fill in for them while they make their annual retreat also tell me, "I would like very much to make one." I have been deeply moved by the earnestness, sincerity, and humble self-knowledge of immense numbers of bishops, priests, and deacons I have known. Catholic priests in the United States seldom put on airs.

The spiritual renewal of the priesthood should focus particularly on the spiritual life and not on sociological and psychological issues. As a psychologist, I must say a *mea culpa* here. In the golden days of psychology, I often blended the popular psychological theories of the moment into my retreats, even though I based them essentially on the spiritual life and particularly on the Gospels. In the 1970s and 1980s, you had to weave things like midlife crisis and self-actualization into retreats in order for anybody to listen. In recent years, I have found that the priests who go on re-treat are much more open to hearing about growth in the spiritual life rather than the sociological, psychological, or even theological issues. Recently, I have been giving retreats on the text "Seek first the kingdom of God and his justice" (Matthew 6:33), and the priest-retreatants are more inter-ested and moved than ever.

The Catholic laity need to encourage priests to be spiritual persons as well as leaders. Often we encourage priests to be social catalysts, to have the answers to many problems, to respond to ev-ery conceivable need. Zealous priests are happy to do this. They have done everything from re-building slums to providing for the chronically handicapped, and these efforts follow the pattern of the saints in the past. The first social worker in history was St. Vincent de Paul, and the first hos-pitals grew out of the infirmaries of the monks, nuns, and friars.

At present, however, priests need to take care of their own spiritual lives. I think a great many of them would hear this call with a sense of joy and relief if only they had the time. Those of us involved in giving retreats for priests — and we are a diminishing band — and those involved in priests' continuing education must seriously evaluate our direction for the spiritual growth of priests and to what extent we are using the classic teachings of the spiritual life. These teachings are well articulated in the documents of the Catholic Church, and two of my books — *Spiritual Passages* (Crossroad, 1982) and *The Journey Toward God* (Servant Publications, 2000) — were written as part of my work with priests. While not at all original, they clearly show the classical teachings of the spiritual life.

This does not imply a rejection of psychology or sociology in the consideration of the priestly office; what is called for, rather, is a central focus on the spiritual life in which other elements become helpful.

No one has ever called priests more frequently and more eloquently to holiness of life and conversion than Pope John Paul II. His apostolic letter *Pastores Dabo Vobis* ("I Will Give You Shepherds") contains a wealth of information and instruction to seminarians and priests on their continuing spiritual formation. Perhaps nothing, however, is as pointed and helpful as the very first letter that he wrote to bishops and priests on Holy Thursday, 1979. As you read these words, they obviously apply to all Christians, but the Holy Father applies them in a special way to priests and their identity. Although almost twenty-five years old, his thoughts are worth repeating as we look to see what can be done for and by priests to restore the reputation of the Catholic priesthood and, more important, its overall spirituality.

In consequence, we must all be converted anew every day. We know that this is a fundamental exigency of the Gospel, addressed to everyone, and all the more do we have to consider it as addressed to us. If we have the duty of helping others to be converted, we have to do the same continuously in our own lives. Being converted means returning the very grace of our vocation; it means meditating upon the infinite goodness and love of Christ, who has addressed each of us and, calling us by name, has said: "Follow me." Being converted means continually "giving an account" before the Lord of our hearts about our service, our zeal, and our fidelity, for we are "Christ's servants, stewards entrusted with the mysteries of God." Being converted also means "giving an account" of our negligences and sins, of our timidity, of our lack of faith and hope, of our thinking only "in a human way" and not "in a divine way." Let us recall, in this regard, the warning that Christ gave to Peter himself. Being converted means, for us, seeking again the pardon and strength of God in the sacrament of Reconciliation, and thus always beginning anew, and every day progressing, overcoming ourselves, making spiritual conquests, giving cheerfully, for "God loves a cheerful giver."

Being converted means "to pray continually and never lose heart." *In a certain way prayer is the first and last condition for conversion*, spiritual progress and holiness. Perhaps in these recent years — at least in certain quarters — there has been too much discussion about the priesthood, the priest's "identity," the value of his presence in the modern world, etc., and on the other hand there has been too little praying. There has not been enough enthusiasm for actuating the priesthood itself through prayer, in order to make its authentic evangelical dynamism effective, in order to confirm the priestly identity. It is prayer that shows the essential style of the priest; without prayer this style becomes deformed. Prayer helps us always to find the light that has led us since the beginning of our priestly vocation, and which never ceases to lead us, even though it seems at times to disappear in the darkness. Prayer enables us to be converted continually, to remain in a state of continuous reaching out to God, which is essential if we wish to lead others to Him. Prayer helps us to believe, to hope and to love, even when our human weakness hinders us.[11]

In his excellent and brief review of the priesthood of our time, *The Priestly Office*, Avery Cardinal Dulles sums it up very well:

> Although all the baptized are called to holiness, that call comes with special urgency to the priest, who represents Jesus the sinless one. Keeping his eyes fixed on Christ, the priest will unceasingly strive to be able to say with Paul, "Be imitators of me, as I am of Christ" (1 Cor 11:1). In the full sense of the word, Christ alone is holy because all other holiness is a participation in his. As Son of God, uniquely filled with the Holy Spirit, he is the pattern of all priestly holiness. As they grow in love for him, priests will rejoice in their vocation and will experience that his yoke is easy and his burden light (cf. Mt 11:30).[12]

One of the effects of the present crisis in the Church has been, as one young priest said to me, "to make us the most squeaky-clean clergy in the history of the world." Things done in darkness have been preached from the rooftops. Not only the guilty and unrepentant but also the long-ago guilty and repentant, as well as the innocent, have paid the price.

Now is the moment to go on with as fervent a priestly life as possible. Priests who are willing to remain faithful, continue with their duties despite a greater shortage of personnel, serve people even in the face of criticism and rejection — these will certainly gain a great blessing from God, the blessing of fidelity, and they will suffer along with Jesus Christ as St. Paul encouraged us to do because He has first suffered for us. Most of the priests who have been deprived of their ministry because of scandal are still able to offer the Mass privately. They can now lead lives of genuine prayer, humility, and devotion, offering intercession for those who have been hurt. This, too, is a vocation.

Reform of Catholic Agencies and Institutions

The same problem that affects Catholic institutions of higher learning — namely, the push to attract more customers — has also deeply affected Catholic agencies and institutions. These agencies were founded by religious who gave of themselves with a great deal of personal self-sacrifice. It was the nuns especially who opened schools, hospitals, orphanages, and agencies for the blind, lame, and aged; and they sacrificed their whole lives to this work, receiving very little of this world's comforts in return. I once surveyed a cemetery in London next to an orphanage run by the Daughters of Charity of St. Vincent de Paul. The tombstones in that little cemetery represented twenty thousand years of religious life. Think of the millions of years of religious life spent by sisters, brothers, and priests in establishing Catholic agencies of welfare and education throughout the United States. We are all too often reminded that a small number of them failed in their vocations. But does anybody think of the immense amount of human labor and sacrifice that went into these agencies of care and charity?

Unfortunately, as government became more and more involved in health care and social agencies, self-sacrificing Christian motivation began to be diluted with concern about just wages — especially for lay staff — as well as profits and plans for endless expansion. I have seen the effects of this change, and for this reason our community of friars, following the example of the Missionaries of Charity of Mother Teresa, resolved that we would accept nothing for the care we give to the poor. Our source of income would be donations given for our support, and nothing would come from what had been given for the poor and the needy.

Catholic social agencies became big businesses, or at least big social operations. The charitable purposes and message of the Gospel often became increasingly obscured over the past forty years. It reminds me of an old English saying: "It was as cold as charity." With some restoration of religious life, and the growing number of dedicated lay apostles, we can hope that the charitable nature of so many Catholic institutions will be restored. Already the spirit of selfless generosity can be seen in the growing pro-life movement, the expectant-mother-care centers, and the care of homeless mothers and children.

But many aspects of the work of Catholic charities, despite the best intentions of their directors and workers, seem unfortunately to have become not very different from those of non-Catholic or nonreligious agencies. This is particularly appalling when Catholic agencies become involved in things that are contrary to the Church's moral teachings. Not long ago, a friend of mine who had received assistance at the ob/gyn program of a large Catholic hospital showed me brochures obtained from the hospital lobby that advertised contraception. This is the sign of a house divided against itself. Even more appalling and almost unmentionable is the rumor that those working for Catholic agencies occasionally encourage unwed mothers to seek abortions. Such behavior moves from disloyalty to abomination.

Those running Catholic social agencies and health care facilities must examine their consciences and make sure they are not pulled into the general paganism of our time. It seems obvious that some housecleaning has to be done. If the sad example of the scandal that has happened in the clergy were to be repeated in social agencies, how devastating it would be, especially for the poor and needy, who rely on these agencies for survival.

A Jewish attorney friend of mine asked me why we Catholics receive such bad press. He said, "You people do more good for everyone than anyone else does. Why are they picking on you all the time?" It is perhaps because we try to do good. We try to keep alive the culture of life. When we cease to do that, we deserve to fall and fail because we have become a sign of contradiction.

The Pro-Life Movement

Without a doubt, the strongest voice against the killing of unborn children in the United States is the Catholic Church. In the vast majority of dioceses, there are faithful Catholics, mostly laypeople, who regularly protest against abortion and offer generous services to help unwed mothers deliver and, if possible, keep their children. The pro-life movement in the United States would certainly be very much smaller and less effective if it were not for the Catholic presence.

The other side of the coin is that in comparison to our numbers and influence, we have been quite negligent. It is not unusual for some dioceses to have only a pro forma pro-life program, and frequently the only ones active in it are laypeople. Where are all the priests and religious? In our community, the sisters and friars regularly demonstrate and pray in front of abortion clinics. It is rare enough to see another priest there, except intrepid souls like Monsignor Philip Reilly of Brooklyn, who is one of the outstanding clergyman in the pro-life movement in the United States. Except for the Sisters of Life and some of the new communities, most of the many religious communities in New York are never seen.

When we remember that on Judgment Day we will be asked what we did against this horror and curse of abortion, it is surprising that Catholics are not far more enthusiastic and clear in their support of the cause of life. We need to be a much stronger and more united voice to protect the innocent. As we have mentioned, according to the statisticians, the gay community comprise only two or three percent of the adult population, and yet they are able to effect much legislation favorable to themselves — some of it justified, some of it not.

How much more powerful could even the minority of actively practicing Catholics in the United States be in the pro-life movement? They would number between twenty million and twenty-five million people, or about ten percent of the population. Such a large cohesive group of voters could have a tremendous political effect. But we do not stay together or speak together for this cause, which is definitely God's cause. Many of my readers would consider themselves pro-life, but I must ask: What you are doing? It is fine to say that you are pro-life, but do you have any impact on the political and social life of the community?

The Holy Father summed up our responsibilities very well in *Evangelium Vitae* ("The Gospel of Life"):

> By virtue of our sharing in Christ's royal mission, our support and promotion of human life must be accomplished through the service of charity, which finds expression in personal witness,

various forms of volunteer work, social activity, and political commitment. This is a particularly pressing need at the present time, when the "culture of death" so forcefully opposes the "culture of life" and often seems to have the upper hand. But even before that it is a need which springs from "faith working through love" (Gal 5:6). . . .

In our service of charity, we must be inspired and distinguished by a specific attitude: we must care for the other as a person for whom God has made us responsible. As disciples of Jesus, we are called to become neighbors to everyone (cf. Lk 10:29-37), and to show special favor to those who are poorest, most alone and most in need. In helping the hungry, the thirsty, the foreigner, the naked, the sick, the imprisoned — as well as the child in the womb and the old person who is suffering or near death — we have the opportunity to serve Jesus. . . .

Where life is involved, the service of charity must be profoundly consistent. It cannot tolerate bias and discrimination, for human life is sacred and inviolable at every stage and in every situation; it is an indivisible good. We need then to "show care" for all life and for the life of everyone. Indeed, at an even deeper level, we need to go to the very roots of life and love. . . .

To this end, appropriate and effective programs of support for new life must be implemented, with special closeness to mothers who, even without the help of the father, are not afraid to bring their child into the world and to raise it. Similar care must be shown for the life of the marginalized or suffering, especially in its final phases.[13]

In the early fall of 1983, Terence Cardinal Cooke, Archbishop of New York, wrote a number of letters calling on people to be true disciples of Christ. His letter in defense of life (dated October 9) is still a classic and is deeply moving because he wrote it with almost the last gasp of his strength. It was actually read in every archdiocesan pulpit on the Sunday after his death. The letter challenges us to be more active and more committed to defending life, as well as avoiding any direct or indirect support for any cause that takes the life of innocent human beings. The greatest scandal in our country right now is the legal death of almost forty million innocent human beings. The voice of the Catholic Church against this infanticide has been weakened considerably by the scandals and the resulting media attack. We need especially to renew our commitment to the Gospel of life. Cardinal Cooke's words are all the more significant now:

It is at times when life is threatened — such as times of serious illness — that the Lord gives us a special grace to appreciate "the gift of life" more deeply as an irreplaceable blessing which only God can give and which God must guide at every step. From the beginning of human life, from conception until death and at every moment between, it is the Lord Our God who gives us life, and we, who are His creatures, should cry out with joy and thanksgiving for this precious gift. . . .

From the depths of my being, I urge you to reject this anti-life, anti-child, anti-human view of life and to oppose with all your strength the deadly technologies of life-destruction which daily result in the planned death of the innocent and the helpless. Together we must search for ways to demonstrate this conviction in our daily lives and in our public institutions. In doing so, we must never be discouraged or give up. Too much is at stake — "the gift of life" itself.

The "gift of life," God's special gift, is no less beautiful when it is accompanied by illness or weakness, hunger or poverty, mental or physical handicaps, loneliness or old age. Indeed, at these times, human life gains extra splendor as it requires our special care, concern and reverence. It is in and through the weakest of human vessels that the Lord continues to reveal the power of His love.

In late April of this year, as the media attack on the Church brought more and more scandals into focus, and as the failures of too many clergy became obvious, many people, including priests, told me they hoped that the Church would be stronger after this was all over. There was a widespread desire that the Church would be purified, that immoral and inconsistent elements in Catholic life would be decimated by the very suffering the scandal had caused, and that we would all be called to repentance and a more fervent Christian life. I can only pray and hope that that is true. It seems to me that the greatest catastrophe would be for us to return to life as usual.

Reforms are difficult to get going, and they are difficult to keep going. The reform of the Church at the time of the Council of Trent did not have the complete support of the hierarchy for almost forty years after the beginning of the Protestant Reformation. Those who dillydallied surely had to answer for it when they stood before the judgment seat of God. We need to move quickly, and we need to move decisively. There is a whole army of fervent young Catholics who are filled with hope. One meets them at colleges, at youth and pro-life activities, and even in high schools. They are even more obvious among the small group of seminarians and younger priests and religious. They all want a dynamic Christianity. When they are exposed to vague and unintegrated forms of Catholicism and the lasting effects of skepticism, they are more fervent than anyone else. This is the time for reform. The bell is ringing in the Church, and remarkably, those who can lead the reform are the young. George Weigel, in his articles on this issue, has summed it up very well:

> This is a spiritual crisis. John Paul II was exactly right in his Holy Thursday letter to priests: these scandals are "grievous" manifestations of the "mystery of evil" at work in the world. The scandals have psychological, legal, and political dimensions. But at the bottom of the bottom line, this is about sin. This is about wickedness. This is about our need for redemption. Unless we understand the crisis primarily in those terms, we are not going to fix what is broken.[14]

If you have read this far, then you are a Catholic, or at least a Christian, who is interested in reform. I encourage you to read the next chapter very carefully. I have tried to think of ways to make this reform effective and real. There are many obvious suggestions and many ways to do it. Unless we think of effective means to start the reform and keep it going, this terrible time of scandal will be wasted suffering. On the other hand, if bishops, priests, deacons, and laypeople — all of us, but especially the clergy — push and work together with a sense of repentance and renewed commitment, then the light of Christ will shine through the Church. Even the victims, who have been left with such a tragic and bitter memory, will see in Christ's words and in His gifts of the sacraments the very things that are necessary for the salvation of us all.

A Choice: Reform or Decline

The noise of the present scandal will die away, leaving its bad effects. The media monster will slither away to attack other victims. We Catholics have a choice. Either we move definitively toward reform or we go back into even deeper mediocrity and confusion. Everyone will have a part to play — from members of the hierarchy to the humblest lay apostle giving out rosaries to the poor. And in the end, all will be judged by what they have done.

It would be very easy to fudge things, to say one thing and to do the other. Some will try to throw a bone to the devout but never really confront the truth of Christ's Gospel in their lives. Some will change and recognize the errors of the immediate past, while others will be lulled into a complacent attitude, smugly secure in the knowledge that we are, after all, the true Church.

These would do well to recall the depth of God's wrath of at the end of 2001 and in 2002. Some will work and pray for reform of themselves and of the Church. And all will proceed at the same rate of speed to the Last Judgment.

Endnotes

1. See *Catherine of Genoa*, trans. Serge Hughes, intro. Benedict J. Groeschel. Classics of Western Spirituality (New York: Paulist Press, 1979).

2. See John C. Olin, *The Catholic Reformation: Savonarola to Ignatius Loyola* (New York: Fordham University Press, 1992), p. 16.

3. George Weigel, "From Scandal to Reform: The Imperative of Orthodoxy," *Denver Catholic Register*, April 17, 2002; see also Appendix II.

4. Ibid.

5. Letter of St. Gregory the Great, "*Sicut aqua frigida*," to Eulogius, Patriarch of Alexandria (August 600) in *The Companion to the Catechism of the*

Catholic Church (San Francisco: Ignatius Press, 1994), p. 148.

6. Rudolf Schnackenburg, *The Moral Teaching of the New Testament* (Burns & Oates, 1982), pp 74-78.

7. *Confessions*, VIII, xi.

8. *The Heart of Newman* (San Francisco: Ignatius Press, 1997), pp. 123-125.

9. I discussed the pastoral problem presented by this group in *With Mind and Heart Renewed*, ed. Thomas F. Dailey, O.S.F.S. (University Press of America, 2001). This volume is in honor of Father John Harvey, founder of Courage. See also *First Things*, June/July 2002, p. 90.

10. *The Ritual Process* (Chicago: Aldine, 1969), p. 106.

11. "Letter of the Supreme Pontiff to All the Priests of the Church on the Occasion of Holy Thursday 1979" (Boston: St. Paul Editions), pp. 28-29.

12. *The Priestly Office: A Theological Reflection* (New York: Paulist Press, 1997), pp. 71–72.

13. *Evangelium Vitae* (1995), para. 87.

14. George Weigel, "From Scandal to Reform: The Nature of the Crisis," *Denver Catholic Register*, April 10, 2002.

Four

REFORM NOW!

The age of dissent, skepticism, moral relativism, and plain old worldliness appears to be under God's judgment right now; and if we fail to respond to this judgment, the Church will surely slip into greater mediocrity and irrelevance. The Church's situation will get worse and worse until there is another and more severe accounting. The catastrophe that has befallen the Catholic Church in the United States and other English-speaking countries is of such magnitude that all loyal Catholics must at this time resolve to work in every way they can for a really thorough, systemic reform — one that will take years to accomplish.

Reform is never easy, because human nature takes the line of least resistance. We must struggle to be united in our determination for reform, and it is especially the responsibility of young adult Catholics to become aware of the issues of reform as well as the means to accomplish it. As I was writing above about the various problem areas, I indicated what I thought would be helpful, such as writing to colleges and cancelling subscriptions to anti-Catholic papers. Now I want to speculate on some larger issues and the strategies to face them.

Getting Good People to See the Problem

The vast majority of Catholics do not see the need for reform in all areas because they are not well-informed. The corrosive effect of the spirit of dissent is only now becoming obvious in the crisis over the sexual behavior of some of the clergy. Ninety-eight percent of the clergy have nothing directly to do with the scandal. Yet, we members of the clergy are also affected by the corrosion resulting from moral relativism, minimalism, skepticism about the teachings of the New Testament, and a general lack of reverence for the Christian tradition and the dogmas of the Catholic faith. If we do not get most priests and people to see this and to act to correct it, there will be no foundation for reform.

Most believers best understand these things in concrete ways, and that is why the spirit of dissent must be seen and identified as nothing less than disloyalty to Jesus Christ. It was never meant to be disloyalty, but that is what it is. Christ said, "He who is not with me is against me, and he who does not gather with me scatters" (Luke 11:23).

Mother Teresa, a woman totally dedicated to the Gospel, gradually brought me to see how far we have strayed from loyal discipleship, and she did this by her example more than by her words. Many other witnesses of reform have also tried to raise a voice for reform and loyal discipleship to Jesus Christ. These include people as different as Dorothy Day, Mother Angelica, and Pope John Paul II; lay leaders such as Jean Vanier of L'Arche and Chiara Lubich of the Focolare Movement; and the founders of new lay and religious communities overseas such as

Father Richard Ho Lung, founder of the Missionaries of the Poor in Jamaica.

The vast majority of people — clergy, religious, and laity — who have contributed to the present weakened state of the Church are almost totally unaware that they have done so. I count myself among them. They never wanted to do this. Indeed, many of them spent most of their time trying to lead a good Christian life despite the confusion arising from moral sloppiness, a failure to identify mortally sinful behavior of many kinds, and the de facto denial that each one of us will stand before the Lord where "he will repay every man for what he has done" (Matthew 16:27).

Fifteen years ago I looked up and realized that I was an unconscious cause of the decline of the community I love so much. Although outspoken, I had in many ways become what Thomas Merton called a "guilty bystander." Unlike many others, I was in a position to try to do something about it; therefore, I would commit a grave sin of omission if I did nothing. It takes only a little bit of courage to look at real decline in the light of day. Unfortunately, we are easily aware of our small failures, which cause us not to see the big ones we are a part of. For that reason, many spend much time, energy, and goodwill rearranging the deck chairs on the *Titanic*.

We have been rudely awakened from our sleep of mediocrity and moral relativism by the so-called pedophilia scandal. We have seen that this is really a homosexuality scandal; but it is also, in fact, part of a much larger scandal of moral relativism. How did the Catholic Church — so well-off, so successful, so well-received by others, and so informed — ever get to the sorry state we see it in now? One is reminded of the words in the Book of Revelation, words so appropriate at this time, where the Lord speaks to the Church in Laodicea:

"I know your works: you are neither cold nor hot. Would that you were cold or hot! So, because you are lukewarm, and neither cold nor hot, I will spew you out of my mouth. For you say, I am rich, I have prospered, and I need nothing; not knowing that you are wretched, pitiable, poor, blind, and naked. Therefore I counsel you to buy from me gold refined by fire, that you may be rich, and white garments to clothe you and to keep the shame of your nakedness from being seen, and salve to anoint your eyes, that you may see. Those whom I love, I reprove and chasten; so be zealous and repent. Behold, I stand at the door and knock; if any one hears my voice and opens the door, I will come in to him and eat with him, and he with me. He who conquers, I will grant him to sit with me on my throne, as I mysef conquered and sat down with my Father on his throne. He who has an ear, let him hear what the Spirit says to the churches." (Revelation 3:15-22)

The Church Intimidated

How did the Church in the English-speaking world — and in fact, in much of Continental Europe — get into its present sorry state? The bishops at the Council worked hard, they prayed fervently, and priests and people enthusiastically supported their renewal. What happened? My guess — and it is only a guess, but an educated one that a number of thoughtful people agree with — is that we became the Church intimidated, the Church led by public opinion, political correctness, popular slogans, and media hype. To use a good, simple biblical term, we were led by the "spirit of the world."

Most contemporary Christians would be hard-pressed even to describe what is meant by the spirit of the world, as it is indicated in the New Testament and in the writings of the saints. They would say that the spirit of the world is the spirit of God. We do not even allude to the words of Christ: "The ruler of this world is coming [but he] has no power over me" (John 14:30); "For all that is in the world, the lust of the flesh and the lust of the eyes and the pride of life, is not of the Father but is of the world" (1 John 2:16); "Be of good cheer, I have overcome the world" (John 16:33).

Modern society lives on slogans and short-term issues, usually produced by media hype. Sometimes, indeed, these slogans and hype serve the best of causes, as they did in the civil rights movement, which was directed against an evil so wicked and so pervasive that you could not miss if you attacked any part of it. We forget that a few decades before the civil rights movement against racial segregation and injustice began, much of the media hype was in the opposite direction. It was pro-segregation.

The hype concerning the Vietnam War and the ensuing peace movement was a bit different. The issues were far more complex. War is always awful, to be avoided at all costs except in the cause of justice, as St. Augustine pointed out in the *City of God*. But wars such as the Vietnam conflict have many sides to them, and anyone who can settle such questions simplistically with a yea or nay is bound to be wrong. I know this because I was active in the peace movement until I discovered that some of my fellow peaceniks were paid agents of the Communist Party. I was being intimidated on all sides and became confused. Then it was revealed that the Bolsheviks were in clear competition with the Nazis for killing tens of millions of people. I was intimidated by an obviously good cause — the cause for peace — but it was presented as a cloak that concealed something very sinister.

I think the same thing may have happened to the Church in the United States.

How Do We Get Intimidated?

If you review the history of this Church called Catholic, or universal, or indeed of other Christian churches — some of which share our antiquity and roots, like the Orthodox Churches and those that came out of the Protestant Reformation — you will find that respected church leaders and the faithful become intimidated by the times they live in. You may recall the great film *Henry V* starring Laurence Olivier, which opens with a bishop trying to justify the land-grab war in France called the Hundred Years' War. This was in every way an unjust war, and it was brought to an abrupt end in one year by a mystic visionary, a young peasant girl named Joan of Arc. Although Henry V was leading an unjust war, no less a person than Shakespeare admired him while at the same time being unsympathetic to the French, who were the victims. It was only when God spoke through the mouth of a little peasant girl, and with the voice of her martyrdom, that the tide of history began to flow "relentlessly against England," as Winston Churchill has written.

Joan was God's messenger, a real historical miracle. Yet, everyone else was intimidated, and most of the intelligent people acted like fools — the English and the French, the clergy and the laity. Today, on the wall of the tower from which St. Joan was led to execution is the document of condemnation signed by a bishop and a score of theologians from the University of Paris. They were all intimidated, and at the end of their lives they would all come to realize what was summed up by an English soldier who stood near the stake as Joan was burning: "Our cause is lost. We have killed a saint."

Since Vatican II, the Church in the English-speaking world has tried to be good, human, kind, and — shall I say it? — as nice as it could be. We have all but denied the existence of mortal sin and the reality of the Last Judgment. We have been absolved by psychology rather than by the blood of Christ. We have substituted therapy (which has its legitimate place) for repentance. We have replaced the teaching of Sacred Scripture and Church tradition with our own opinions, and we have substituted the evening TV for the pronouncements of the Pope. We have wasted the Church's vast patrimony, built up by poor Catholic immigrants of the past, and splurged the resources they left for the spread of the Gospel on foolish and self-indulgent things. We have given away scores of colleges, hospitals, and other amenities. We have failed to preach and encourage chastity in and before marriage, as well as in entertainment. Now we have harvested the bitter fruit in a shameful and deeply painful scandal.

We must get beyond reacting, and begin proacting. We must preach first the kingdom of God and His justice and then all the things we need as a Church will be given us.

Unless we are convinced that the ultimate truth for salvation and for the guidance of our lives is to be found in our one Teacher, Jesus Christ, we deserve to fail completely as the true Church. And we will. Because of the Holy Spirit's presence, we cannot become the false Church, but we can become the wrong Church, wrong in our attitudes and deeds, like much of the Church on the eve of the Protestant Reformation.

Once we are convinced of the need for reform, the most effective way to understand what we can do is to look at the different roles we have to fulfill according to our vocations. Let me make one observation just for openers, as we say in New York. Reform is now just a little plant, but it will grow; and the Gospel moving in time will define more clearly what must done in the future.

The Laity

One of the popular slogans of Vatican II was that "the Church is the people." I wish! The fact is that the great majority of laity are more traditional and devout than they have been permitted to be by those who saw renewal as the principal object of Christian life.

I have never heard a single layperson complain that the architecture of their parish church was too old-fashioned or too traditional. I have heard endless complaints that beautiful sanctuaries have been destroyed, and that new churches are ugly, undevotional, or simply hideous. I have never heard a layperson complain that Mass was too devout, but I have heard endless bitter complaints that the liturgy was casual, irrelevant, and celebrated in a style that was just plain silly. Even when it comes to the tough teachings on chastity,

I have never had anyone complain about my preaching them. The priest scandal, however, has brought out plenty of frustration, as did the opposition to secularized sex-education courses and the failure to affirm chastity in Catholic education and even in some seminaries.

What can a devout Catholic layperson do? Plenty. *Talk, write, suggest, implore.* When worse comes to worst, threaten — nicely, of course. We shouldn't support anything we morally disapprove of. And a person can withhold support from something that may be far from what they have a right to expect, even though it may not be precisely morally wrong.

But we must always recall that we are talking about a Church and not about a political party. Respect, understanding, truthfulness, kindness, and especially charity are necessary when registering disagreement or disapproval. It often happens that laypeople feel so ignored, frustrated, or patronized that they get angry. Most thinking laypeople have caught on to the old progressive slogan "Ask 'em what they want, but give 'em what they need." That's over.

The establishment of lay boards to evaluate accusations of sexual abuse by clergy can be a real step toward taking the laity seriously. Is an accusation credible, or is it simply frivolous? Are there circumstances when a fallen priest may return to some duties after sincere repentance? A lay board can decide these things well. Parish councils and diocesan councils have so far not been very effective because Catholic clergy and laity are not familiar with this form of procedure, but we seem to be getting better. The simple truth that the real participants in any activity should be heard (for a number of reasons) is beginning to dawn on people.

The next step after this is properly called "collegiality" — a catchall word for the obligation to work together. For our purposes, it means loyalty to the practical working out of Church teaching in very specific circumstances. A number of writers such as Russell Shaw have suggested that what is needed right now are collegial bishops.

Shaw gives a penetrating analysis of the different models used by bishops to live out their difficult roles in recent decades. He demonstrates the need for different models of collegiality among bishops as well as the spiritual component behind this concept, which is communion. While any abstract set of answers to real problems always depends on the responsible living out of these principles, Shaw makes a good case for a new emphasis on collegiality and communion, and for restoring the role of the Pope and the bishops and effective unity. The Holy Father himself put it very well when he spoke at the Synod of Bishops in October 2001: "Only if a deep and convinced unity of the pastors with the successor of Peter is clearly discernible . . . can we give a credible reply to the challenges that come from the present social and cultural world."[1]

Having worked for decades with parish priests, I strongly feel that collegiality must include parish clergy and area conferences; and in the parish, it must include the active and devoted laity. All interested and involved Catholics should have an opportunity to express their hopes, aspirations, and opinions.

Another example here might be helpful. When we began our little reform community, we determined to have a chapter — a monthly meeting of all friars in final vows. This body is consultative rather than legislative, but it gives all permanent members of the community a chance to have a voice. A very fine canonist who assisted us with our constitutions wanted to drop this democratic structure, since it was not provided for by canon law. We pointed out how important it was for us to hear everyone's opinion, even if the friar did not participate in legislative decisions. The chapter is much like a parish council. The canonist phoned back and said, "You are right. I have been in religious life thirty years, and I have never had a chance to express my opinion in a public forum." The laity need to be heard, and they need to speak in responsible and informed ways. If they are not informed, they have a right to be informed.

Among the laity right now there may be reformers like the two St. Catherines (of Siena and of Genoa). We have already had Dorothy Day and Catherine Doherty (Baroness de Hueck) in our time. We have mentioned a few well-known lay reformers outside the United States, as well as new reform movements among the laity in Europe. Let's hope that we hear from some in the United States in the near future.

The Clergy

The destructive effects of moral relativism and the spirit of dissent have eroded the effectiveness of many Catholic clergy. While the overwhelming majority of clergy are completely innocent of the abuse of minors, we must admit that we have been unknowingly guilty of other things. We may have been too intimidated to preach the Gospel, especially the Gospel of faith, hope, and charity. Despite the best of intentions, we may be part of an overall religious mediocrity and not realize how many sins of omission we will face at our particular judgment. We may be lacking in prayer, reverence, zeal, love for the poor and needy, and evangelization. We may be negligent in recognizing the occasions of temptation and sin, especially those found in the media. We may fail to show enthusiasm for the Gospel of Christ and for the Church. At times, we may resemble the hired hands in the Gospel more than we resemble the good shepherds. In his first letter to priests, Pope John Paul II reminded us that we need to examine our conscience and render an account every day.

Recently, a young priest attended a clerical event at which he happened to end up at a table with priests twenty-five years his senior. He told me later that he was disappointed and discouraged by the cynicism and bitterness he heard reflected in the conversation. I happened to know the priests who were at the table, and I reassured him that they were very good men and dedicated to their calling. What the young priest was hearing was the sound of disappointment and frustration. The Church that the older men had entered as seminarians years before had changed radically, and so had the society around them. Unfortunately, the Church has tended to be intimidated by that society. These priests may have been disappointed also because some of their worldly expectations were not fulfilled. They would not have acknowledged that their expectations were worldly, but they were piously worldly. When they entered the priesthood, it was considered a premier vocation, a very high calling — indeed the highest — and it enjoyed tremendous respect from the Catholic community, which then was much closer to its immigrant roots than it is now. Since things did not turn out as these priests had hoped, they were cynical and disappointed. I also happen to know that these men pray, and that they are sincere, generous, and in their own way quite dedicated. But they have been jaded by the fact that we live in an intimidating situation. They themselves feel intimidated.

Being intimidated is like being trapped. It is one of the unhealthiest psychological situations that people can get themselves into. There are men and women who have been imprisoned for many years for the faith who did not feel trapped while they were in prison. There are others who have felt trapped living in a rather comfortable rectory. A lot depends on your attitude, and your attitude depends on how well and how often you pray to Jesus Christ.

During the years I have worked with priests, there has been a good deal of interest in what is called spirituality. Often it was a spirituality watered down, rather than strengthened, by psychology and sociology. The successful priest was evaluated more by social norms than by anything else: What did he do to mobilize people? How popular was he in the parish? How was he as a social catalyst? Was he able to build and add to things?

Americans are suckers for success. So, when the success was tangible and worldly, a man was thought to have achieved things. This was all the more true if he achieved those things because of some conflict with the diocesan authorities. Somehow, people began to admire those who were in conflict with authority. This often reflected the spirit of dissent.

About twenty-five years ago, when many priests were leaving, I recall that if you went to a meeting of priests, those who had left were treated as if they were heroes. They were spoken of as if they had acted with great courage in giving up their vocation. Others were admired because they had "stood up" to the Pope or to Rome or to whomever. This included a number of well-known theologians and scholars. The dissenting priest-professor was the hero *par excellence* no matter what he said.

That spirit of dissent is now very much up for judgment. Through prayer and spirituality, some priests who are dissatisfied retain a real devotion to Christ as our one Teacher. Although they may disagree with those in charge of the Church, they will not do so in a way that betrays a kind of underlying enjoyment at being a bad boy. Others will come to the conclusion that dissent was the only way out of the Church's problems, and they will probably leave the Church. In fact, I would not be surprised to see a number of priests leave their vocation in the next year or two. The spirit of dissent that pervaded the Church for so many years has now been found guilty of leading us into the moral mess in which we find ourselves at the present time.

A book that is illustrative of the spirit of dissent and of relativism was quite popular with some members of the clergy in the past year. This book, which I reviewed in *Inside the Vatican* (November 2000), is *The Changing Face of the Priesthood*, by Father Donald Cozzens. The author was the rector of St. Mary's Seminary in Cleveland at the time he wrote the book. Without going into all that the book says — and a few things are well-said — it can be considered "Exhibit A" in what was wrong with American seminaries.

There is much discussion of psychology, with many references to Freud and Jung, but very few to the Fathers and Doctors of the Church. When the Pope is quoted, it is in a largely negative context. But there are long pages on psychoanalytical techniques that are now passé. What is most disturbing in the book is the extensive discussion of homosexuality among the clergy. I asked a very bright priest, who had been a successful financial officer of a corporation in the past, to read the book and tell me if he saw one indication of disapproval of homosexuality or of homosexual behavior on the part of priests. He could find no disapproval, nor could I. It should be noted that Father Cozzens does clearly condemn pedophilia.

People are surprised when I say that I am pleased that this book was written. It gives the strongest evidence and clearest illustration of what the spirit of dissent and moral relativism has done to undermine Catholic seminaries. It happened that three seminarians from St. Mary's were on retreat at our Trinity Retreat House shortly after

Father Cozzens' book was published. The only word to describe their disagreement with the book and their rage was *incandescent*. They felt deeply betrayed by the book, and in no way accepted its premise that homosexual activity of any kind was consistent with the Catholic priesthood. They strongly took issue with the premise that many seminarians are homosexual.

When the media's feeding frenzy against the clergy was at its height, I was very pleased that a reporter approached me to do an interview regarding the current scandal. An article appeared in the New York *Daily News* (April 7, 2002), which was balanced and fair. It placed before the public several important facts: sexual abuse by members of the clergy is not an exclusively Catholic phenomenon, nor is it in any way as pervasive as the media in general have led people to believe. The media, moreover, have chosen to exploit the current crisis affecting the Catholic priesthood because of the Church's opposition to abortion and its refusal to accept homosexual liaisons as equivalent to marriage.

Without the slightest hesitation, I can say that I am honored to be a member of the Catholic priesthood at the present time. Innumerable good priests struggling successfully with all kinds of temptations and difficulties in the present morally decadent anticulture are proving themselves to be Christ's true disciples and loyal members of the Church. My question to these priests is: What can we do to move things in the right direction in the Church?

I strongly suggest a renewal of personal spirituality. For the moment, let's forget the biblical criticism (often skepticism in disguise), theological speculation, psychology, and sociology, and get down on our knees and speak to our Lord Jesus Christ from the depths of our heart. He is our model, and we are His servants. Priests and bishops — and indeed all Christians — should bring themselves before Christ and try to imitate His example. The experience of Christ in the soul of a believer is much more real than any theory.

Some years ago an anthology of St. Augustine's homilies on the ministry was published, with an introduction by Michael Cardinal Pellegrino, a renowned Augustinian scholar, to commemorate the sixteen-hundredth anniversary of the saint's conversion.[2] For the most part, these homilies were preached at the ordination of bishops and focus on the relationship between the good shepherds and the hirelings (see John's Gospel, chapter 10). Bishops are warned not to be like the hirelings!

Augustine cites the relevant Gospel passage: "The good shepherd lays down his life for the sheep. He who is a hireling and not a shepherd, whose own the sheep are not, sees the wolf coming and leaves the sheep and flees; and the wolf snatches them and scatters them" (John 10.11-12). He comments:

> The hireling plays a bad part here and yet he is not entirely useless; he would not be called a hireling unless someone employed him and paid for his services. Who, then, is this hireling, who deserves reproach but is also indispensable? . . . In the Church, there are certain people in positions of authority of whom the apostle Paul says, "They seek their own ends, not those of Jesus Christ" (Phil. 2:21). What does it mean, "They seek their own ends"? It means that they do not love Christ for nothing, they do not seek God for the sake of God; they pursue worldly rewards, their eyes are fixed on gain, and they long to be honored by their fellow creatures. One in authority who loves such things and serves God for the sake of them is a hireling and not to be reckoned among the children of God. Our Lord says of such people, "I tell you truly, they have received their reward" (Matt. 6:5).[3]

St. Augustine, a realist among realists and always aware that the Church was a field sown with wheat and weeds, never denied that hirelings were necessary. He points out that St. Paul even speaks of the hirelings: "Some indeed preach Christ from envy and rivalry, but others from good will" (Philippians 1:15). St. Augustine writes:

> Christ is truth; let truth be proclaimed in pretense by hirelings and in truth by the children of God. The children patiently wait for their Father's eternal inheritance; the hirelings are in a hurry to get their worldly reward from their employer. As for my own human glory, which I see the hirelings envy, may it decrease, and may the divine glory of Christ be proclaimed far and wide by the tongues of both hirelings and children of God, since Christ is proclaimed both in pretense and in truth.[4]

St. Augustine goes on with his description of hirelings in ways that could make many of us pause to examine our own consciences. He writes:

> Who is the hireling who sees the wolf coming and takes flight? The one who seeks his own ends, not those of Jesus Christ, and does

not dare accuse the sinner openly (1 Tim. 5:20). Here are some who have sinned, and sinned gravely; they ought to be rebuked, they ought to be excommunicated, but excommunication will turn them into enemies who lie in wait and do harm whenever they can. The one who seeks his own ends, not those of Jesus Christ, is already silent and refrains from reproach for fear of losing what he pursues — human friendship — and of incurring the vexation of human enmity. Here was the wolf seizing the sheep by the throat, the devil persuading the faithful to adultery, and you keep silent instead of reproaching; you hireling, you saw the wolf coming and you fled. He answers indignantly: Look, I am here, I have not fled. You fled because you were silent; you kept silent because you were afraid. Fear is mental flight. You stood in body but fled in spirit, which was not the action of the one who said, "Though absent in body, I am with you in spirit" (Col. 2:5).[5]

With all of this, what does St. Augustine say of the good priest or bishop? The following words actually describe the office of bishop, but they also fit the priest very well.

We must reproach the restless, encourage the timid, support the weak, confute our opponents, beware of the treacherous, teach the ignorant, rouse the lazy, restrain the contentious, check the proud, make peace among the quarrelsome, help the needy, free the oppressed, approve the good, tolerate the bad, and love all. In this great, many-sided, and varying office with its different concerns, you must help us with your prayers and your obedience, so that we may delight not so much in being set over you as in being useful to you.[6]

Following the example of St. Paul, who constantly asked people to pray for him, St. Augustine encourages people to pray for those whom God has set over them. He ends with the words: "If we continually pray for you, and you for us, with perfect Christian love, then with our Lord's help we shall happily come to eternal blessedness."[7]

In these confusing times, it is essential for every priest and seminarian, as well as every bishop, to keep constantly before his mind that he is in this role for the salvation of souls. His cultivation of the spiritual life and progress on the journey can of course be part of the fulfillment of his own reason for existence. But the added dimension of serving the People of God and calling them to holiness should be paramount in the eyes of the priest. What a magnificent and beautiful vocation it is to live, labor, and give oneself so that people may be saved through Christ. How awful it is when that vocation is squandered, and one realizes in the gray light of dawn that one has acted like a hireling. But this is an opportunity for penance.

It is wonderful to see so many fervent, dedicated young men and women coming into the priesthood and religious life. They are not great in numbers, but they are great in zeal and fervor. They are the hope of the Church. They often face discouragement, or even scandal, misunderstanding, and reproach from those who see their zeal threatening the mediocrity of the past. Sometimes their fervor and loyalty are seen as obstacles to their vocations by seminary staff riddled with the spirit of dissent. I often wonder whether Voltaire should not be named the patron saint of seminary personnel. His attitude was well summed up in his motto "Anything but zeal."

In a few years, the fervent young people will be the leaders of the Church. I pray that they will continue in their present zeal and conversion, and that skepticism and cynicism, which are the work

himself, may not impede what they are
to do in the Church for its reform.

Members of Religious Communities

Much of what I have said about priests is true
of religious as well. But religious have certain
unique responsibilities of their own. Religious life
obligates its members to strive for an ever fuller,
more complete self-dedication to follow Christ,
to observe His commands and counsels, and to
embrace the work or responsibility that Divine
Providence puts before them as individuals. I have
always been uncomfortable with the phrase "strive
for perfection." It seems Pelagian to me, and it
appears to ignore the fact that by reason of original sin we can never be perfect. However, my problem was an obsessive-compulsive interpretation
of "perfection." The word really means complete,
making no exceptions. This is Our Lord's obvious
meaning when He speaks about forgiveness and
tells us, "You, therefore, must be perfect, as your
heavenly Father is perfect" (Matthew 5:48) and
"He makes his sun rise on the evil and on the good,
and sends rain on the just and on the unjust"
(Matthew 5:45). "Perfect" means complete, and
striving evermore for the complete giving of self
to God.

Religious life is dying because it has become a service of self, of one's own comfort and fulfillment. The question is always asked: What can religious do? Let's rephrase the question: What are we obliged to do? What must we do if we are not to fail in our vocation and compromise our relationship with God, and even compromise our salvation?

A certain complacency and profound denial grips religious life of men and women in the English-speaking world. People will tell you that everything is going fine, even though their communities are fading into oblivion. Religious are not only rearranging the deck chairs on the *Titanic*, but they are also planning to throw a party next week as the water pours through the portholes.

Let me say again that I am aware there are an immense number of good religious sisters, brothers, and priests. Most of them, however, are frustrated, frightened, and despondent about any future for religious life. The few young religious around who do not belong to the rare communities that are growing spiritually are completely disillusioned by what they see. Is there a way out of this?

The only way is through courage and bravery. People need to stand up at chapters, local meetings, and even in ordinary conversations and say that we must get back to basics. We have lost the basics. Even one serious step toward recovering the basic purposes of religious life and its observances would lead to a revival of the others. Those who are unwilling to go along with the basic steps should be left for the moment in their own orbit, but in due time they have to be pulled in, too. They will resist in every conceivable way because religious life has become an opportunity for them to lead a very comfortable life, have security, and avoid paying income taxes. If you think that this is an exaggeration, ask yourself how many religious actually pray and attend the liturgy of the Eucharist every day. This should be the minimal prayer life of a religious.

Religious could take such basic steps as returning to the community's apostolate, to common prayer, and to the common life. Any one of these steps would spark such an earthquake that the religious life would begin to come back itself. One substantial step would pierce the eggshell, so the new little chick of a reborn religious community could emerge.

One wonders whether this can happen. I have seen a few abbeys and provinces of long-established men's communities begin to move in the right direction. They simply started by keeping the basic observances of religious life, and the result was almost like a landslide. When you run into these communities year after year, you see their greater fervor and observance and much greater joy. Most long-established communities are still in the doldrums, but they often have enough younger members who are dedicated to the reform of religious life to bring about a renewal in the next few years, unless they are completely thwarted.

In the other communities, unfortunately, reform will not occur and devout religious will continue to be isolated. The members who remain will have the vocation of giving their community a Christian burial. I do not wish in any way to minimize the importance of that vocation. If the community is dying, let its members at least see to it that it die with dignity and prayerfulness, even if they have to stand alone.

Who Writes the Will?

An important issue — and one of some urgency — faces religious communities, the hierarchy, and the Holy See. Many of these communities still have large property holdings and even substantial amounts of money. The last few sisters and brothers alive are going to be the richest people in the state. These funds belong by right to the

Church's apostolate. They were given by the faithful to support religious life, Catholic education, and other Catholic services. Unfortunately, as I have mentioned in connection with education, the purpose of these funds has been ignored, and the funds themselves have been alienated from the Church's apostolic works. It will be an incredible scandal if this happens with the final resources of religious communities.

There should be a forceful endeavor to outline the proper disposition of the remaining funds and patrimony of religious communities as they die away. Otherwise, there will be a grab for these funds, which will bring even more opprobrium to a situation involving the appalling but ignored scandal of the alienation of Catholic colleges and universities from the Church's apostolate.

Religious need to raise their voices. When we finally come to be judged by God, we must remember the words of Jesus: "So every one who acknowledges me before men, I also will acknowledge before my Father who is in heaven" (Matthew 10:32). Obviously, this has to be done in a kindly and charitable way, but it also has to be done directly and uncompromisingly. Put "kindly" and "directly" together, and you had better do it with a sense of humor as well.

Religious life is intimidated to death in the United States and in the English-speaking world. That's why religious gave up their religious garb and common life and a common apostolate. The absurdity of adult men and women religious who are living an entirely secular life — in apartments and other dwellings, wearing entirely secular clothes, and doing entirely secular work — must be exposed. This is a grave abuse for which individuals must answer on Judgment Day. Those who support these abuses do not like to hear these words; they are putting their heads in the sand, and perhaps endangering their own salvation and that of others.

It has been stated that religious life cannot be lived in our culture in its traditional way, which is a statement I reject absolutely. The experience of our little community and of a number of other new communities flatly contradicts this observation. For example, the Franciscans of the Renewal, fifteen years old at this writing, have about eighty members between the friars' and the sisters' communities. About three-quarters of these are still in formation, and there is constant growth. The smaller new communities have more vocations by far than the larger, older ones, which are dying but cannot admit it.

If you are a religious in a dying community and you are in a position to do something, you are obliged to do it. Don't let anyone tell you anything else. You will be accused of divisiveness, uncharitableness, and all sorts of other things. Better to be accused by men than to be accused by Christ of failing to live up to your vocation. I would welcome the opportunity to debate in public, at any time and under any circumstances, those who wish to disagree with these observations. (I'll even pay for my own carfare.)

I hear from many elderly religious who are despondent and hurt by what has happened to their communities. They are often deprived, without proper canonical authorization, of even having a vote in the community because they are "retired." This deprivation may also violate their civil rights as U.S. citizens. Religious write to me about severe violations of canon law and even of violations of directives of the Congregation for Institutes of Consecrated Life and Societies of Apostolic Life, which go on persistently. Extraneous issues like the environment preoccupy the minds and reading of many religious, while they are busy pointing out the problems of others. Religious men particularly, whose communities have been undermined by the clerical gay scene, have the most

serious obligation to speak out and work for reform. Those who are too old to do anything else
must pray and be as observant as possible.

I have seen many examples of elderly religious
maintain their integrity and honesty in the midst
of a chaotic scene. Of course, they were laughed
at or rejected, but it scarcely bothers them. They
had made enough progress in the spiritual life so
that the criticisms of others meant little or nothing to them.

Perhaps people once entered religious life
without much sense of obligation, but because of
the attractiveness of the vocation based on secondary motives like the prayer life, the community life, or some other good. The motive for
becoming a religious must be that I believe that
Christ has called me as an individual by His Divine Providence and through the inspiration of
the Holy Spirit to undertake this way of life of
prayer and service sanctified by the saints and
ennobled by its history. Religious should read over
the history of their community and ask whether
they are upholding or betraying the tradition of
the brave people who founded their community
centuries ago. We were chosen by Divine Providence to live in this time; and because we live in
a time of decline and scandal, we have every

obligation to fulfill our Christian vocation in the face of these dark realities. But "if God is for us, who is against us?" (Romans 8:31).

The Bishops

It is with reluctance that I take up the topic of what bishops can do in response to the scandal of our time. My reluctance is motivated by three things.

First, I have an ingrained respect for the authority of bishops as successors of the apostles, which was given to me by the exemplary religious and fine priests I knew. It was not a superstitious respect; in the Catholic community, we all knew long ago of the faults, shortcomings, and foibles of bishops. In fact, they were often the subjects of a certain amount of humor, most of which was very good-natured. However, the respect for the office of bishop as successor of the apostles was there. A bishop is an unfortunate priest who has been chosen by Divine Providence to have this very heavy responsibility.

The second reason for my reluctance is that I have some idea of the difficulty of being a bishop or religious superior in these times. For the last twenty-five or thirty years, anyone who has been in a role of high authority in the Church has been navigating on stormy seas. I am not exonerating the bishops even for being intimidated, but simply pointing out that we all have to get over being intimidated. Bishops and major superiors, like most other people, were intimidated because the situation was very intimidating. It was new and unprecedented. Without a good grasp of Church history, a bishop found himself almost without models.

Third, I am somewhat reluctant to write about what bishops should do because I know they are unjustly judged by people; in the media, from right to left, they have been made the whipping boys of the situation. There is no doubt that some bishops and religious superiors have made serious, even egregious errors. Some have given grave scandal, and others are victims of false accusations. No doubt, some have paid more attention than they should have to lawyers and people in the behavioral sciences. It is also obvious that bishops, wishing to do their job as best they could from their point of view, have proceeded from attitudes that could be popularly termed liberal, conservative, or middle-of-the-road. If these are a bishop's honest attitudes, he can do nothing but follow them with caution and prayer. There are a number of bishops who will very much disagree with what I say in this book. I understand their disagreement, because they are operating from their own frame of reference. I respect their right and need to differ, but they must also respect my need to appraise the situation from my point of view as best I can.

That being said, let's admit the fact that the role of bishop and major superior has been much too identified with and influenced by the image of the chief executive officer of a major corporation. Although there are administrative responsibilities and similarities, the image of the CEO is very far from the one presented by Christ, who says to Peter, "Feed my lambs. . . . Tend my sheep" (John 21:15, 16). St. Paul tells the bishop to be a pattern to the flock.

My observation that bishops and major superiors should not act like CEOs will puzzle a number of people, including some in these positions. The CEO-bishop suggests a secular role imposed on a more important and essential role, one assigned by Christ Himself in the Gospel. If we know our Church history, we know that the mistake of bishops' adopting a secular role has been made before. In medieval times, bishops became the "lords spiritual," corresponding to earthly rulers, the "lords secular." Anglican bishops to this day sit in the House of Lords. There were even prince-bishops. I suppose the ultimate confusion of roles was that of the Pope as sovereign of the Papal States.

As democracies replaced medieval feudal structures, bishops looked for different models. Since Vatican II, that model has become the CEO. The same is true of major superiors of religious men and women. Although anyone in authority at this time must have serious administrative responsibilities, these should never come close to eclipsing the pastoral care of clergy, religious, and especially the laity.

There were always bishops who did this, often in the face of a majority who followed models and experience drawn from secular society. For instance, while bishops took on the external trappings of medieval society, there were always those who went against the tide and were more pastoral and Gospel-oriented and who avoided the trappings of nobility. One thinks of St. Anselm (Archbishop of Canterbury), St. Norbert (Archbishop of Magdeburg), and St. Bonaventure (Bishop of Albano). The latter told the messengers to hang the newly arrived cardinal's hat on a tree while he finished doing the dishes. We also recall St. Louis (Bishop of Toulouse) and the sixteenth-century reformers St. John Fisher (Bishop of Rochester) and St. Charles Borromeo (Archbishop of Milan);

it was St. Charles Borromeo who made the reforms of Trent a real part of Church life. Later still we have St. Francis de Sales (Bishop of Geneva) and, in the United States, St. John Neumann (Bishop of Philadelphia). In the past century, examples include St. Pius X and Blessed John XXIII, both of whom wore the papal honors very lightly.

Would anyone think of John Paul II as a CEO, pulling his old frame from place to place to bring a message of peace and reconciliation? In my time, I have seen bishops who were devout CEOs and very dedicated. But my image of a great bishop is mostly inspired by a man who was a capable administrator and yet a humble friend and brother to thousands. Both Catholics and non-Catholics thought of him as their personal friend. I speak, of course, of the Servant of God Terence Cardinal Cooke.

A few years ago, a friend of mine who became a diocesan bishop told me after the annual bishops' meeting that he never wanted to go back again. There was nothing bad at the meeting, but it proceeded very much along the lines of a business organization. Another young bishop, who had spoken out about what both he and I saw as an abuse, was later called aside by one of the most esteemed and respected prelates in the United

States and pleasantly admonished: "That's not the way we do things here." It was all done as between "gentlemen," but nonetheless, as we used to say in Jersey City, "He was given the shiv" — that is, the dagger. In other words, he was told to behave himself.

This explains why so much that is wrong in the Church has not been looked at. Consequently, so many of the abuses we have discussed in this book, quite beyond the issue of sexual misbehavior, have continued to grow and weaken the Church, causing a deplorable loss of respect for its authority. Bishops above all are to be patterns of the flock and must avoid the spirit of dissent. While a diocesan bishop is a teacher in the Church, he is above all a member of the universal Church. In the West, he receives his office directly from the Bishop of Rome and is obligated to be loyal not only to the Church's teaching Magisterium but also to the Pope. It is well known that among the bishops in the United States and Western Europe there are a few very sad and obvious dissenters from papal authority. But there is a larger number who through their silence not only fail to uphold traditional Church teaching but also give consent to what may be contrary to that teaching.

It is distressing to observe that priests who are publicly known to be dissenters are at times appointed bishops and even diocesan bishops. The same is true at the elections of religious superiors who are dissenters.

In the case of bishops, a set of questionnaires, or scrutinies, are sent to a variety of people, seeking to determine whether someone is capable and appropriate for the office. The questions in these scrutinies, I am told, raise issues of the candidate's orthodoxy, loyalty, and his avoidance of dissent concerning Church teaching. Obviously, people are not telling the truth when they fill out these scrutinies. This greatly disedifies many of the clergy and laity, who are hoping for bishops who will support the ordinary Magisterium of the Church and its supreme bishop. One may disagree with the Pope or with the bishops of a country at proper times and in legitimate ways. There are saints who have done this, but not in matters of faith and morals. Saints have stood up to popes, but always to defend the orthodoxy of the Catholic faith or morality. St. Catherine of Siena, who stood up to a pope, was a reformer, not a dissenter.

Anyone becoming a diocesan bishop at the present time deserves a great deal of sympathy from friends and relatives. It is an almost unendurable task, complicated immensely by cases of clerical misbehavior and other failures, which we have outlined in this book. Any bishop trying to do a reasonably good job — and the vast majority are — deserves our compassion and support. For this reason, when devout Catholics wish to bring to the attention of a bishop or a major superior the failures in the life of the Church that have occurred on his watch, they must do so in a respectful, patient way.

The best way to approach episcopal authority is first to go up the line of command leading to the bishop. This must always be done with what is called a "paper trail." It is far better to send a well-thought-out and well-written observation and proposal to someone in ecclesiastical authority. The proposal is best if signed by several people who represent a broad base of support in the community —- for example, professional people such as physicians, educators, businesspeople, and even well-known benefactors of the Church. A note scribbled in longhand on loose-leaf paper will not accomplish much, even though it may be written very much from the heart. If you are going to make your voice heard, take the time and have the patience to write a letter reflectively and responsibly.

A bishop or a major religious superior, on the other hand, must be open to receiving and learning from criticism, or at least from divergent points of view. It's wrong to dismiss people simply because they have a different way of looking at things, and this is true whether they are seen as too liberal or too conservative. At times, people have to be admonished because of the excess of their views or the manner in which they express them. But they deserve a hearing. If nothing else, this will assist the bishop or major superior in growing in that elusive Christian virtue — humility. I don't think it is at all unwise for a bishop or superior who is receiving severe criticism to say kindly to the person, "Would you like to be in my situation? Could you have some respect for my feelings, because I am trying to do my best?" Most people are decent enough to respond well to such a personal appeal. People do not respond well, however, to being ignored or patronized.

Bishops and major superiors of religious orders must look squarely at the problem of dissent. We have written enough about the climate of dissent and its corrosive effects. Dissent is often an expression of what may be called "false teaching," a phrase borrowed from Reginald Cardinal Pole, the last Catholic Archbishop of Canterbury. Cardinal Pole was a reformer, and his mother — St. Margaret Pole, Countess of Salisbury — was a martyr under King Henry VIII. Cardinal Pole strove to restore order to the Church and only missed being a martyr himself by his untimely death. He was one of the loudest voices demanding reform from the time of Luther's break with the Church to the Council of Trent, which opened twenty-eight years later (1545). That delay in itself is a scandal in Church history. When Cardinal Pole addressed the Council, he told the bishops that they needed to accept responsibility for the Protestant break with the Church of Rome. He said that the bishops were responsible for three reasons: they had failed to condemn false teaching, which then led to heresy; they had failed to condemn public immorality; and they had failed to condemn the land-grab wars of Europe.

It is worthwhile to look at Cardinal Pole's distinction between false teaching and heresy. A hundred times when I have spoken up and objected to strange, unusual, inconsistent ideas and teachings that did not integrate at any honest intellectual level with Catholic tradition, I was told: "Oh yes, but they are not heresy." They may not be heresy now, but they may lead to heresy in the future.

When the Cardinal finished telling the bishops at the Council of Trent what they needed to hear, he then invited them in a touching way to take upon themselves the guilt of the situation, as Christ had taken on the guilt of the world. The following thoughts, when we realize the circumstances in which they were said, are deeply moving and pertinent:

> Therefore what in his great love of God the Father and his mercifulness towards our race Christ did, justice itself now enacts of us that we should do. Before the tribunal of God's mercy we, the shepherds, should make ourselves responsible for all the evils now burdening the flock of Christ. The sins of all we should take upon ourselves, not in generosity but in justice; because the truth is that of these evils we are in great part the cause and therefore we should implore the divine mercy through Jesus Christ.[8]

During the recent crisis, a great deal of anger and disappointment has been directed toward the hierarchy. Much of this is the result of media hype and manipulation, but some of it is not. I have experienced it with my own relatives, who are good Catholics.

No other procedure would settle the situation more powerfully than an apology from the clergy and the hierarchy as well as an admission that serious mistakes have been made. I think that this must go quite beyond the area of the so-called pedophilia cases. The Church must accept some responsibility for the alienation of Catholic universities, colleges, and agencies. We must acknowledge responsibility for the deplorable deficiencies in Catholic education and also for the collapse of religious life. The Pope has apologized often. The American clergy ought to consider the possibility.

The idea of truth has, unfortunately, been compromised in the United States by the media, public relations schemes, and what is (and is not) considered politically correct. What the people long to hear now is the truth, and they will want the truth comprehensively. It cannot be told piecemeal here and there.

Right now, nothing would restore confidence in the episcopate better than a firm stand against pornography, extramarital sex, abortion, euthanasia, and the general moral decline of the United States. Tough topics like contraception and autoeroticism need to be consistently and publicly addressed. Sure, people will leave the Church, but most of them in fact have left already. Many Catholics who criticize the Church severely in the media haven't practiced the faith in years. It's hypocrisy for them to call themselves Catholic. Some others will leave the Church now. We clergy can't compromise the Catholic faith or morals, tolerate an erosive dissent, and still say that we are taking care of God's flock.

Because of this scandal and many other things, the Catholic Church in this country is moving back into the ghetto and resuming the status of a minority group. The ghetto can be a protection, a strength. It can cause great identity and is not necessarily a bad thing. One man's ghetto is another man's hometown. We will never be as we were before the Second Vatican Council; we have too many friends in other religious denominations and too much involvement in the ongoing life of the country. But we need to restore our identity, and no groups are more responsible for that than the U.S. Catholic bishops and the major superiors of religious orders. Long and fervent prayer and acknowledgment of mistakes are absolutely necessary for this reform to begin.

The worldly nun St. Teresa of Ávila marked the beginning of her conversion and change, which led to such immense good over the centuries, from the time she began the practice of prayer. We must practice prayer — fervent, deep, self-confrontational prayer. It doesn't have to be interesting, nice, or consoling. But it must bring the truth of the Gospel into our lives in an uncompromised way.

And we must pray for the whole Church. Any wise and loyal Catholic is praying fervently for bishops. Such labels as liberal and conservative have become almost meaningless in the present crisis, because people from every side should realize that we have all contributed to the erosion of Catholicism and the confusion of Catholic identity. Perhaps there are different ways to express this reform and a method for returning to a strong Christian identity. Time and prayer will tell. We must be true to who we are — and this applies to each of us on an individual level. I once heard someone say, "Be true to yourself, because if you deny yourself, you have nothing left." All those reading this book would describe the first and most important characteristic of their personal being as their faith. If we are not true to our faith, we are dishonest all the way through.

Crossing the Threshold of Hope

Our Holy Father began the third millennium with a call to cross the threshold of hope. We must have great hope right now — not hope in men or in our institutions or even in our best institutions, but hope in the Holy Spirit, that He will give us the grace to follow His inspiration and be loyal to His gifts. Then out of this chaos and darkness, this Calvary, will come a victory for the Church over evil. Otherwise, the Church will continue to disintegrate.

Hope is an essential Christian virtue. The Church has been in these difficult circumstances before, as it was on the eve of the Protestant Reformation. Those who stood by the Church in the past and spent their lives working for reform, often with a great deal of opposition from people in the Church, show us the best way of preserving the Catholic faith in modern times. If God asks us to spend our lives doing this, we should be honored to do so.

There once was a young layman, an unaccomplished person, and for a time rather irresponsible in a nice, friendly sort of way. The Church in his time was very much in control but in desperate need of reform. In fact, he grew up just before a great reform council. Suddenly the young man felt called by God, not to reform the Church but to try literally to follow the Gospel way of life. Jesus Christ, dead and risen more than a thousand years earlier, suddenly became real to him, especially in the poor and the outcast. He listened to the Holy Spirit. He ran impetuously and with youthful abandon along the way of the Gospel. Many thought him a fool, unrealistic, and headstrong.

But he had a secret. He took God absolutely seriously. He followed the Gospel without compromise. He attracted followers without actually wanting or trying to do so. He ran along the way of the Gospel, and his life sparked a great reform. How would he look in the contemporary Church? Many would think him a fool, naïve, fundamentalist, anti-intellectual, or irrelevant. But this young man became the great reformer of his time, and he still intrigues hundreds of millions of people.

St. Francis of Assisi has much to teach us about faith, unworldliness, spontaneity, mercy, compassion, self-denial, penance, humility, and acceptance of humiliation. There are many great reformers in Church history, and only a few of them are mentioned in this book. But when I see the totally unexpected and unprecedented spirit of reform in very young Catholics and other Christians of our time, I am forced to conclude that St. Francis has something very special to say to our troubled times. He can be for all of us a model of Gospel reform.

Endnotes

1. Quoted in "The Very Model of a Modern Bishop," by Russell Shaw, *Crisis*, May 2002, p. 33.

2. St. Augustine, *"We Are Your Servants,"* trans. Audrey Fellowes, ed. John E. Rotelle, O.S.A. (Villanova, Pa.: Augustinian Press, 1986). This book is no longer in print.

3. Ibid., p. 21.

4. Ibid., p. 25.

5. Ibid., p. 27.

6. Ibid., pp. 52-53.

7. Ibid, p. 53.

8. Hans J. Hillerbrand, *The Reformation in Its Own Words* (London: SCM Press Ltd., 1964), p. 463.

EPILOGUE

Does all this scandal shake your faith in the Church? I hope so, because ultimately your faith should not be in the Church. Ultimately our faith is in Jesus Christ, and we accept the Church. We support the Church. We believe in and belong to the Church because Christ established it on His apostles.

Someone who belongs to the Church as a world organization, as a great philanthropic movement or the worldwide social catalyst or patron of the arts is going to be badly shaken. Some may get out.

We belong to the Church as the crucified body of Jesus Christ. If the Church is the body of Christ, don't be surprised that it's crucified. Don't be surprised that it's betrayed, dragged through the streets, and spat upon and wounded and crowned with thorns. That's what's going on right now. The Church is the body of Christ. And when you love the Church, you should love it as the body of Christ.

Our beloved Holy Father, on Good Friday 2002, wrote this:

> In the acute pain of the Suffering Servant we already hear the triumphant cry of the Risen Lord. Christ on the Cross is the King of the new people ransomed from the burden of sin and death. However twisted and confused the course of history may appear, we know that, by walking in the footsteps of the Crucified Nazarene, we shall attain the goal. Amid the conflicts of a world often dominated by selfishness and hatred, we, as believers, are called to proclaim the

victory of Love. Today, Good Friday, we testify to the victory of Christ Crucified.

Not so long ago, the Catholic Church seemed to be very triumphant. I lived through those days at the end of the Second Vatican Council. The Church seemed to be very powerful. I've lived to see the mystical body of Christ crucified, betrayed, attacked — and abandoned by the frightened apostles. And we're all part of it. Don't ever exempt yourself. I reproach myself every day that unwittingly I went along and stupidly I got involved in things that ultimately did not serve the Church or Christ so well.

Now is a time to move on wisely and well. We may be a leaner, cleaner, and more attacked Church, but Christ will be with us. His word will be heard, His sacraments given and received with devotion and humility, and His holy doctrine and teaching will be embraced. All this can happen if we embrace His cross, which has come on the Church in such a strange and unexpected way. Now is the time to turn to God.

PRAYERS

The following prayers have been composed primarily for the use of the people indicated in each title. However, they are also meant as meditations for others. Specifically, the prayers are to be said by those who have been victims and those who have been the sinners, but they are also meant to be read by others. My goal in writing these prayers is not only to help individuals who need them but also to assist the rest of us in gaining some insight into how those hurt by this scandal experience life in this very difficult time.

Prayer for the Church in Time of Scandal

Lord Jesus Christ, You have called blessed those who "are not scandalized" in You. You referred to those who could be shocked or distressed by Your apparent inability to ward off evil, and especially during Your own Passion. In fact, You sent these words to the imprisoned John the Baptist, by way of his disciples who came to ask if You were the

Holy One or whether they should look for someone else. And John died a cruel death, and You wept. And people asked whether You, who had done such miracles, could not help him.

Lord, do not let us be scandalized or shocked or shaken in our faith by Your apparent weakness in this time of trial for Your Church and people. Some of Your disciples have failed You very badly, and some have been confused and hesitant in their response to evil. And some have been deeply wounded and hurt by the failure. We have nowhere else to go and can turn only to You, with an urgency born of faith and trial. Give grace to Your Church and Your people so that we will not fall away. Help us to carry out whatever we can and must do in order to root out the causes of scandal, to make up for whatever part we may have contributed by not speaking up, by not giving good example, and by not preaching Your Gospel in all that we say and do. We ask You to deliver Your people from this scourge and to heal the wounds of the Church so that we may emerge from this darkness more committed to You, more honest, more penitent, and more open to Your grace. We pray to You, Christ our Lord. Amen.

Prayer to Be Said by Victims and Their Families

O Lord Jesus Christ, crucified so long ago for our sins and by our sins, You are the supreme Victim, the Victim of sin and abuse, the Victim of cruelty and heartlessness. You are the Victim of the treachery of Your own disciples. They say You are still crucified in those who suffer today. I feel betrayed by someone who spoke to me in Your name, who may even have given me the sacraments. I am confused, angry, and disheartened. I don't even know how I can believe. But whom shall I come to if I don't come to You, for You alone have the words of everlasting life.

You have promised to send us Your Holy Spirit, to strengthen, to console, and to give us wisdom. I don't even know if I want these gifts. I want to go off to a corner, forget who I am and what I am called to be — a child of God. I want to turn away in bitterness, maybe even laugh at the whole message. But something keeps me here looking to You: it is a faith that goes beyond what men do, a hope beyond what they can promise. I believe and I hope only because it is given to me to do so by Your grace.

I wish I could write off what has happened simply as incredible human weakness and the failure of a human being to live up to what he was called to be. Maybe I can forgive and cope with the fact that I was not protected by those who should have done so. Perhaps I have looked into the face of evil, of a man who should not have been born. But I can't remain here.

Jesus Christ, my Savior, You went on when all was darkness. When Satan called all his legions to defeat goodness, You overcame him with love and forgiveness. You prayed for those who were killing You.

I do not have such charity and forgiveness in my heart. So I ask only for the grace to move on, to do good and avoid evil in my life. Help me to take one good step at a time. Perhaps someday, with Your help, I may be able to live as fully as I am called to live. Maybe someday I will understand and be able to forgive. For now, Lord, help me to do what I can do, really and sincerely. Help me to take the first steps, to get on with my life, to wish to forgive, if that is possible. Someday I may be able to join Your prayer of forgiveness from the cross. But do not let me cling to my wounds. Help me to get over them and go beyond them, to use my wounds — a victim's wounds — to be part of the healing that You, the Divine Victim, brought to the fallen human race.

Prayer to Be Said by Priests Who Sinned Against the Young

Note: I wrote this prayer in the very early hours of the morning, after much prayer to the Holy Spirit. Into it I have woven the thoughts and words of priests I have known who have been sinfully involved with teenagers. Most of what I have written are ideas that they have expressed to me about themselves. The prayer is published here so that you might have some insight into how some of these priests feel at present.

Lord Jesus, You chose to entrust Your word and sacraments to the trembling hands of mortal men. Why did You ever allow me to be one of these? You call weak human beings to carry on Your work. You often entrust Your work to those who are unable to do it, and they are unaware of their limitations. You allow tyrants and despots to rule over nations. You even allow the Church to be persecuted and to fail. You permit it even to be misled. You even allowed a traitor to be one of Your disciples, and You chose weak men who would fail You in Your hour of suffering to be the founders of the Church. You permitted me, who would betray You in this awful way, to be the dispenser of Your sacraments and word. I must confess in the clearest possible way that I have been a bad priest. But often I tried to do good, good that is all in question now. You have warned us that those who did what I have done would be better off if they had not been born. From the depths of my being, I cry out for any person I have hurt, especially the young, for my victims — individuals and their families. Do not let them suffer anymore because of me. Heal the wounds I have caused, and if it helps, put these wounds on me.

Even if I sinned out of great weakness, out of driven madness, I take complete responsibility for my actions. You never turn away from anyone. You called Judas Your friend. I deeply need Your merciful grace if I am to have even a shred of hope. I accept all the punishment I receive, even what I see as unjust, precisely because I have been most unjust.

Merciful Savior, give my victims, their families, and the people I have scandalized the grace of healing. And give me a hope of salvation.

I may have lost everything — my priesthood, my life, my good name, my security, and even my freedom — but do not, I beg You, let me lose my soul. I have hurt the young, the innocent, and the people who cared about me and loved me. I have nothing left but my hope in Your merciful forgiveness. That is all I have along with my shame. Lamb of God, who take away the sins of the world, have mercy on me and on us all. Amen.

Prayer to Be Said by Those in Charge
(Bishops, Superiors, and
Their Assistants)

Lord Jesus Christ, Founder and Shepherd of the Church, I have accepted the responsibility of serving in Your name. Perhaps at times I have given in to the temptation of thinking I was important, that without You I could do anything. Perhaps I have forgotten that we all pass like shadows through this world, and that the only good we do derives from the fact that You act in us. I regret that fear, human respect, and intimidation have motivated my actions. I repent that I have not always allowed Your Gospel to be my guide and the Holy Spirit to be my Counselor. I regret my weakness, which I never saw because I did not examine my conscience carefully enough. I regret that I was often so anxious to listen to the flock that I did not hear You — the Shepherd. I repent that I have not acted with as much care as I might have toward the victims, their families, the People of God, all those hurt by this scandal, and even those who failed so badly in their vocation.

Deliver me from fear, hesitancy, and self-indulgence, and from being guided by the spirit of the world that has nothing to do with You. I repeat the words of the first among the apostles: "Lord, save me. I am perishing."

Help me, O Lord, to do my assigned task in the Church, whatever it may be and for as long as You wish. Give me the grace to be patient at the failure of others, honest in the fulfillment of justice, merciful in dealing with all, and prudent in the discharge of my duties.

Keep me from seeking my own advantage. Rather, by the Holy Spirit, help me, poor sinner that I am, to serve Your people, especially the victims and the scattered flock, as best I can. For Your sake, let me accept anger and wrath directed against the Church because You have suffered and died for me.

Help me to take up this cross every day and follow You. And give me the grace always to believe that by Your holy cross You will bring good out of evil. Amen.

Prayer to Be Said by Those Falsely Accused

Lord Jesus Christ, my heart is bitter and my life almost unbearable because I have been falsely accused. Although I am a poor sinner completely dependent on Your grace for my salvation, I am innocent of what I have been accused of. Help me to regain my composure, to forgive my accusers and their allies, to calmly defend myself without a rancor and bitterness that will leave me guilty. Help me to be truthful, open, and wise in what I say. Give me Your Holy Spirit to keep me from panic and rage. Most of all, help me to trust in You, that at the end You will bring good out of evil, even for me. I pray for my accusers that they may be converted from evil intent or false judgments.

Lord, You remained calm before Pilate, in Your hour when You were falsely accused. Help me in this trial to do all things as You would have me do them and to trust in Your justice and mercy. Amen.

APPENDIXES

Appendix One

POPE JOHN PAUL II

The following is the text of an address by Pope John Paul II to the American cardinals at the Vatican, Tuesday, April 23, 2002.

A Papal Address to the Cardinals of the United States

Dear Brothers,

1. Let me assure you first of all that I greatly appreciate the effort you are making to keep the Holy See, and me personally, informed regarding the complex and difficult situation which has arisen in your country in recent months. I am confident that your discussions here will bear much fruit for the good of the Catholic people of the United States. You have come to the house of the Successor of Peter, whose task it is to confirm his brother Bishops in faith and love, and to unite them around Christ in the service of God's People. The door of this house is always open to you. All the more so when your communities are in distress.

Grief at scandal, sense of solidarity with victims and families

Like you, I too have been deeply grieved by the fact that priests and religious, whose vocation it is to help people live holy lives in the sight of God, have themselves caused such suffering and scandal to the young. Because of the great harm done by some priests and religious, the Church herself is viewed with distrust, and many are offended at the way in which the Church's leaders are perceived to have acted in this matter. The abuse which has caused this crisis is by every standard wrong and rightly considered a crime by society; it is also an appalling sin in the eyes of God. To the victims and their families, wherever they may be, I express my profound sense of solidarity and concern.

Establish better criteria to avoid mistakes, uphold need for conversion

2. It is true that a generalized lack of knowledge of the nature of the problem and also at times the advice of clinical experts led Bishops to make decisions which subsequent events showed to be wrong. You are now working to establish more reliable criteria to ensure that such mistakes are not repeated. At the same time, even while recognizing how indispensable these criteria are,

we cannot forget the power of Christian conversion, that radical decision to turn away from sin and back to God, which reaches to the depths of a person's soul and can work extraordinary change.

Neither should we forget the immense spiritual, human and social good that the vast majority of priests and religious in the United States have done and are still doing. The Catholic Church in your country has always promoted human and Christian values with great vigor and generosity, in a way that has helped to consolidate all that is noble in the American people.

A great work of art may be blemished, but its beauty remains; and this is a truth which any intellectually honest critic will recognize. To the Catholic communities in the United States, to their Pastors and members, to the men and women religious, to teachers in Catholic universities and schools, to American missionaries in all parts of the world, go the wholehearted thanks of the entire Catholic Church and the personal thanks of the Bishop of Rome.

Fidelity to Church teaching on matters of sexual morality, care in selecting candidates

3. The abuse of the young is a grave symptom of a crisis affecting not only the Church but soci-

ety as a whole. It is a deep-seated crisis of sexual morality, even of human relationships, and its prime victims are the family and the young. In addressing the problem of abuse with clarity and determination, the Church will help society to understand and deal with the crisis in its midst.

It must be absolutely clear to the Catholic faithful, and to the wider community, that Bishops and superiors are concerned, above all else, with the spiritual good of souls. People need to know that there is no place in the priesthood and religious life for those who would harm the young. They must know that Bishops and priests are totally committed to the fullness of Catholic truth on matters of sexual morality, a truth as essential to the renewal of the priesthood and the episcopate as it is to the renewal of marriage and family life.

God can purify the Church through this trial

4. We must be confident that this time of trial will bring a purification of the entire Catholic community, a purification that is urgently needed if the Church is to preach more effectively the Gospel of Jesus Christ in all its liberating force. Now you must ensure that where sin increased, grace will all the more abound (cf. Rom 5:20). So

much pain, so much sorrow must lead to a holier priesthood, a holier episcopate, and a holier Church.

God alone is the source of holiness, and it is to him above all that we must turn for forgiveness, for healing and for the grace to meet this challenge with uncompromising courage and harmony of purpose. Like the Good Shepherd of last Sunday's Gospel, Pastors must go among their priests and people as men who inspire deep trust and lead them to restful waters (cf. Ps 22:2).

I beg the Lord to give the Bishops of the United States the strength to build their response to the present crisis upon the solid foundations of faith and upon genuine pastoral charity for the victims, as well as for the priests and the entire Catholic community in your country. And I ask Catholics to stay close to their priests and Bishops, and to support them with their prayers at this difficult time.

The peace of the Risen Christ be with you!

Appendix Two

GEORGE WEIGEL

The following excerpts on dissent and the need for reform are taken from a four-part series titled "From Scandal to Reform," which originally appeared in the Denver Catholic Register, *in the Spring of 2002, in Mr. Weigel's column "The Catholic Difference." They appear here courtesy of Mr. Weigel. The full text of the columns is available online at the Ethics and Public Policy Center website (www.eppc.org).*

Excerpts From the Series
'From Scandal to Reform'

Dissent

. . . A culture of dissent has been a staple feature of Catholic life — sometimes blatantly overt, sometimes less obvious — since the birth control controversy of 1968. In recent years the culture of dissent has been more subtle, as reforms of seminaries and diocesan offices have been undertaken with some success. But the habit of dissent has been hard to break. Indeed, one of the stranger features of contemporary Catholicism in America is the branding of self-consciously orthodox younger clergy and scholars as "ideologues" who are to be consigned to the margins of Church life.

I've met my share of sometimes overly zealous younger priests, academics, and activists, and I understand that orthodoxy has to be combined with pastoral sensitivity, intellectual openness, and prudence. But I also understand that these younger Catholics, committed wholeheartedly (if sometimes clumsily) to the Church's teaching in its fullness, are not part of the problem that has been made painfully manifest in recent months. Their commitment to the fullness and liberating beauty of orthodoxy is part of the solution. . . .

Dissent must be confronted far more vigorously. When seminarians and priests are sent subtle signals that a less-than-enthusiastic acceptance of the Church's teaching on marital ethics, or on homosexuality, or on the impossibility of ordaining women to the ministerial priesthood can be tolerated, corruption inevitably follows. It does not follow universally. It may not even follow in the majority of cases. But that it does follow, and with lethal results, is now self-evident from the evidence with which we have all been bludgeoned these past three months or so. This must change, now.

Orthodoxy is not a problem. Orthodoxy is the key to the solution.

Need for Reform

... For twenty-three years now, in his Holy Thursday letters to priests and in numerous other homilies and addresses, Pope John Paul II has been proposing a noble vision of the priest as an icon of Christ in the world. That vision has attracted thousands of young men to the seminaries; it has reinvigorated the ministry of priests who have been ordained for decades; and it gives the Church the theological substance with which to accelerate the reform of its ordained ministry.

The generation of dissent in the theological guild is greying and intellectually sterile, unable to reproduce itself. Younger scholars, more interested in exploring Catholic orthodoxy than in deconstructing it, will increasingly fill seminary faculties and university schools of theology.

Priests formed in the past fifteen years and committed to the heroic model of the priesthood proposed by John Paul II are eager to be catalysts of reform and renewal.

What is needed now are the bishops capable of leading the reform of local presbyterates, diocesan vocations offices, local and regional seminaries. Some of those bishops have already been ordained and are doing heroic work. ...

The bishops capable of leading the reform the Church needs will be evangelists and pastors, capable of communicating their passion for Christ to their priests and people. There is, arguably, too much raillery about the Catholic bureaucracy today; many Church bureaucrats are entirely admirable people. Yet eighty years after Max Weber dissected the character of bureaucracies, it should be clear that the typical bureaucratic cast of mind — which emphasizes efficient management and damage-control, and almost always prefers amelioration to necessary confrontation — can be in serious tension with the bishop's duty to teach, govern, and sanctify.

Apostles, not managers, are what will move the Church from crisis to reform. . . .

The fully adequate response to today's crisis is the response that is always necessary when the Church is bottoming out — the call to holiness must be lived more intensely by every member of the Church. Everyone. The crisis of today is like the crises of the past. It is a crisis caused by an insufficiency of saints. That is a wake-up call for all of us.

"Crisis" also means "opportunity." The opportunity before all of us is to live holier lives.

Appendix Three

JAMES O. CLIFFORD, SR.

The following is the text of an opinion piece by James O. Clifford, Sr., which was published in Catholic San Francisco, *May 3, 2002. Mr. Clifford lives in Redwood City, California, where he is the founder and only member of Project Medusa (Media Education Drive-U.S.A.). Used with permission.*

Double Standard in Stories About Sexual Abuse

What I want to share goes back 15 years or so when I first realized that the church scandal was a story that had legs, that it was going to take on a life of its own and start walking.

I had just switched from United Press International, a once-powerful news organization that had fallen on hard times, to the rival Associated Press. I wasn't at AP long before an incident occurred that showed me what to expect in the handling of the scandal. It was so long ago that I can't recall all the details, but the San Jose Mercury News had printed an extensive story about suits filed against the church from coast to coast.

The Mercury story didn't bother me. The shock came not long after, when an educational organization held its convention in San Francisco. One of the topics on the group's agenda was sex cases involving public school teachers and the possible legal ramifications. I thought this would be a good story in light of the Mercury's story, particularly because it was the group, and not a newspaper, that was making the matter public. The AP didn't cover it, my boss telling me, "Let's see what the locals (meaning the local papers) do with it." Well, the locals didn't touch it, the AP didn't use it, and the rest of the nation didn't learn about it.

This experience served as a microcosm of the way the story would be played out. My complaint isn't that the church is under attack. It should be. But teachers, who have charge of children more than anyone except parents, seemed, as a calling, to have escaped unscathed.

When the priest scandal took off like a rocket, I expected the teacher troubles to follow the same path. What I saw was a double standard grow and grow, to the point that I started saving stories involving teachers, usually accounts relegated to briefs, given one day runs, or kept off the AP main wire by being isolated in their dateline states.

Oh, yes, there would be the occasional well-covered titillation story. In the main, however, the stories were treated as minor, even though the respected professional publication Education Week regarded the problem as so important, it ran a lengthy series on the subject. The mainstream media seemed to dodge the issue.

In March the influential Washington Post ran a story of at least 1,000 words on the church scandal. One of the best I've seen and very fair, the story pointed out how hard it is to come up with valid statistics in the matter. The story was printed in the San Francisco Chronicle and carried a headline that read in part: "Catholic clergy not alone in having problems."

"They are finally getting around to teachers," I said to myself before I read the story. No such luck. It mentioned scandals involving clergy of other faiths and even alluded to coaches and scout leaders. Not a peep about teachers.

For years, I have tried to learn the reasons for the disparity in coverage. Could it be an anti-Catholic bias? I could have easily reached that conclusion when I read the Chronicle on St. Patrick's Day, one day before that newspaper used the Post piece. Chronicle religion writer Don Lattin penned a long story that informed readers that

"The scandal that won't go away is back and bigger than ever."

Lattin reported that experts who study the clergy say the scandal is about secrecy, power, and control. Well, I've studied the news business, and I say the same thing about sex stories involving teachers. I know there are differences, and I expect strong media reaction to what I write here. But the stories are overwhelmingly similar in that they concern minors and people who misuse positions of trust. I am sure one of the things my critics will point to is the cover-up angle. With teachers, no cover-up is needed. The press is doing it for them. I don't feel Catho-phobia is the main problem — shoddy journalism is. That is, if one feels the role of the media is to inform rather than influence, or that reporters should know a good story when they see it and not first have to be run over by the rest of the journalistic herd.

Recently a teacher was charged in a sex case in Sonoma County. Rohnert Park high school teacher Brant Gaskill was accused of performing sex acts with a 17-year-old student. In addition, he allegedly used a survey in an attempt to learn sex practices of his young charges. If you lived outside of Sonoma County and blinked, you would have missed this story. I heard a brief report on television, then waited for a more detailed account in the Chronicle. I'm still waiting, despite several messages to Chronicle reporters urging that the story be covered. I later found a story in the Santa Rosa Press Democrat, but it did not use a roundup approach mentioning other cases involving teachers.

More important, none of the papers I read or any of the newscasts I listened to carried a very significant Associated Press story on a U.S. Supreme Court hearing in March. The court refused to review a Virginia case in which a teacher's victim sought damages from the school district. The teacher, Craig Lawson, is serving a 30-year sentence. Even though the victim was abused as early as the sixth grade, it appears there will be no "deep pockets" when it comes to school districts.

The AP noted that the case went before the court "as the Roman Catholic Church deals with a scandal involving decades of unreported molestation by priests." I think unreported would also apply to teacher sex cases, as in "unreported" by the press.

Appendix Four

JOHANN CHRISTOPH ARNOLD

*Johann Christoph Arnold is a pastor, marriage coun-
selor and author of ten books, including* Sex, God,
and Marriage *and* Endangered: Your Child in a
Hostile World *(available at 1-800-521-8011 or
www.plough.com). Arnold was elder of the Bruderhof
Communities from 1983 to 2001, and continues to
be its principal author and public spokesman. The
Bruderhof communities number more than twenty-
five hundred souls in ten communities in the United
States, the United Kingdom, and Australia. Based
especially on the Sermon on the Mount and Acts
(chapters two and four), members give up private property, holding all property in common; vow to live
celibately or in lifelong faithful marriage; and vow to
renounce violence (including any form of military service). The Bruderhof's roots are in the early Church
and the communal Anabaptists of the Radical Reformation. The Bruderhof seeks active contact with other
movements for justice, peace, and purity.*

Clergy Sex Scandals Steal Headlines From Countless Faithful Who Defend Children and Uphold Chastity

There is nothing more horrible than child abuse. Jesus said of those who lead children astray, "It would be better if a millstone were hung around their necks and they were thrown in the sea." But the recent scandal surrounding certain Catholic priests should not be allowed to obscure the clear teachings of Jesus about sex, to which millions of Christians, especially in the Catholic Church, strive to be faithful.

Amid this flood of negative publicity, Christians need to take back their faith from those who wear its clothes but don't live it, and publicly witness to what our faith teaches and what we believe — that no one is closer to God than children, and that our bodies are temples of God, fashioned in his image, to be kept pure by abstaining from sex outside of marriage.

I am not Catholic, but my book *Sex, God, and Marriage* (formerly titled *A Plea for Purity*) is widely used by Catholic educators and religious. The first edition enjoyed the enthusiastic support of Mother Teresa, who wrote the foreword, and of Pope John Paul II. Several cardinals have since endorsed it. In thirty years of speaking out for chastity, and for faithfulness in marriage, I have found no other church that advocates such a clear stand on sexual purity, or a leadership so concerned about the direction of our society in this regard. This is what should be making headlines. Our society owes it to the tens of thousands of priests who faithfully serve God and their people.

As a marriage counselor I know what self-discipline it takes for most people to remain faithful in marriage. It must take even more conviction and commitment to remain true to a vow of lifelong celibacy, as priests promise to do. Jesus said of celibacy, "Let those accept it who can."

The problem of pedophilia is not limited to these publicized incidents. The world is full of pedophiles and child abusers, many of them married and close relatives of the abused children. The media, the public, and especially all Christians should remember the words of Jesus: "Whoever is without sin should cast the first stone." Rather than condemn the Catholic Church wholesale because of the hypocrisy of a few, we need to tackle child abuse at its roots — in our legalized pornographic, sex-crazed culture, and in particular when children are used as sex objects in advertising and entertainment. What basis do we have for finger pointing, when so much that we tolerate in our society undermines the standards we would have others uphold?

Any priest who breaks his vow of celibacy and engages in any kind of sexual abuse must be taken to task for his action. Beyond that, however, our concern for the safety and moral well-being of every child should drive us to reaffirm — not attack — the teachings of the Church regarding human sexuality. And to nurture in our own lives the reverence for life on which they are grounded.

FOR MORE INFORMATION

This book had its beginning in three lectures that were given at St. Casimir's Church, Yonkers, New York, on April 17, 2002. The lectures themselves are available on audiocassettes as well as CDs from:

The Franciscan Grassroots Renewal Project
119 Eagle Street
Brooklyn, NY 11222
(718) 349-7622

A donation to cover costs is requested.

Videocassettes are available from EWTN at 1-800-854-6316.

Notes

Notes

Notes

Notes

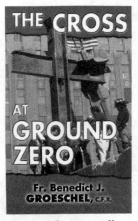

How could God allow such evil in the world? Does God really want His people to suffer? And what do we do now? When vicious terrorists attacked America on September 11, 2001, we all had questions we couldn't answer.

With profound insight and compassion, Father Benedict Groeschel, C.F.R., shows us that God is still very much with us — now more than ever. We may never completely understand why horrible things happen. But we do know that Jesus did not come to take away suffering. He came to sanctify suffering by His presence. He was there at Ground Zero at the World Trade Center, and He will be with us in our time of trial. The steel cross found in the ruins leads straight to the redeeming Cross of Christ. For everyone who has struggled with questions of faith in this time of crisis, this book is a sympathetic companion and guide.

The Cross at Ground Zero
1-931709-30-0 (No. T17), paper, 144 pp.

Available at bookstores. MasterCard, VISA, and Discover customers can order direct from Our Sunday Visitor by calling 1-800-348-2440. Order online at **www.osv.com**.

 Our Sunday Visitor
200 Noll Plaza
Huntington, IN 46750
1-800-348-2440
e-mail: osvbooks@osv.com

Availability of books subject to change without notice.

A29BBABP

We all know that because the Church is made up of human beings, human weakness and sin are at times a reality. This pamphlet, by Lorene Hanley Duquin, helps Catholics understand what to do when someone is hurting. It offers suggestions for healing and forgiveness. It helps these Catholics deal with the anger, resentment, and feelings of betrayal that inevitably arise when they or someone they are close to has been hurt by a member of the Church.

When Someone Is Hurt by the Church
1-931709-59-9 (No. P5)
Available in packages of 50 pamphlets

Available at bookstores. MasterCard, VISA, and Discover customers can order direct from Our Sunday Visitor by calling 1-800-348-2440. Order online at **www.osv.com**.

 Our Sunday Visitor
200 Noll Plaza
Huntington, IN 46750
1-800-348-2440
e-mail: osvbooks@osv.com

Availability of products subject to change without notice.

A29BBABP

Our Sunday Visitor . . .
Your Source for Discovering
the Riches of the Catholic Faith

Our Sunday Visitor has an extensive line of materials for young children, teens, and adults. Our books, Bibles, booklets, CD-ROMs, audios, and videos are available in bookstores worldwide.

To receive a FREE full-line catalog or for more information, call **Our Sunday Visitor** at **1-800-348-2440**. Or write, **Our Sunday Visitor** / 200 Noll Plaza / Huntington, IN 46750.

- -

Please send me: __A catalog
Please send me materials on:
__Apologetics and catechetics   __Reference works
__Prayer books   __Heritage and the saints
__The family   __The parish
Name_____
Address_____Apt._____
City_____State____Zip_____
Telephone (   ) _____
A29BBABP

- -

Please send a friend: __A catalog
Please send a friend materials on:
__Apologetics and catechetics   __Reference works
__Prayer books   __Heritage and the saints
__The family   __The parish
Name_____
Address_____Apt._____
City_____State____Zip_____
Telephone (   ) _____
A29BBABP

- -

Our Sunday Visitor
200 Noll Plaza
Huntington, IN 46750
Toll free: **1-800-348-2440**
E-mail: osvbooks@osv.com
Website: www.osv.com